GOSPEL-TELLING

The Art and Theology Of Children's Sermons

By

RICHARD J. COLEMAN

WILLIAM B. EERDMANS PUBLISHING COMPANY
GRAND RAPIDS, MICHIGAN

To
The Children of the Christian Center
and
My Own Three Children: Joy, Sharon, and Laura

We gratefully acknowledge permission to use the following:

"Devils are no good, you know that, don't you?" from Janwillem van de Wetering's *The Empty Mirror* (Boston: Houghton Mifflin, 1974; London: Routledge & Kegan Paul, 1974).

"A Drop in the Bucket" from *For Heaven's Sake* by Helen Kromer, copyright © 1961 by Helen Lenore Kromer and 1963 (new material added) by Walter H. Baker Company.

Library of Congress Cataloging in Publication Data

Coleman, Richard J.
  Gospel-telling: the art and theology of children's sermons.

  Bibliography: p. 133.
  1. Preaching to children. 2. Children's sermons.
I. Title.
BV4235.C4C64   1982   251   82-11435
ISBN 0-8028-1927-3

CONTENTS

PREFACE

In this handbook my purpose is *not* to provide the minister or religious educator with the usual thirty to forty object lessons or children's sermons. My goal is to help the pastor create his own gospel stories by sensitizing him to what constitutes a good children's sermon and by illustrating the methodology outlined here with a variety of homilies. The ideas and themes of sermons are always more appropriate if they flow from the minister and his own particular situation. If this handbook succeeds, it will do so not because of any great originality on my part but because I have managed to impart my belief that within each of us is an unlimited source of creative ideas that can be developed into meaningful gospel messages for children.

According to my experience, most books of children's sermons are filled with good examples of what goes wrong when we try to communicate the Good News to children. In no way is it sufficient for ministers to tell children cute moralistic stories or preach adult sermons reduced to a child's level. The former runs the danger of substituting good behavior for the Good News, and the latter overlooks the fact that children live in their own world and cannot be considered miniature adults.

It is equally unacceptable for ministers and teachers to resort to rephrasing biblical narratives or dressing up those "old favorites" in modern styles. Unfortunately, the false assumption persists that there is a certain sanctity and sanctification in mastering the traditional biblical stories—e.g., Noah and the ark, David and Goliath, Zacchaeus and the sycamore tree. The consequence of this approach is a congregation of adults who still do not understand and still have not internalized the real meaning of these stories.

Next to the crucial issue of moralizing the Gospel, I am most disturbed by the lack of sound theological thinking in that part of the worship service which includes children. On those rare occasions when I have found a children's sermon worth repeating, I have sorely missed the theological reasoning behind its selection and creation. Without sound theological principles we can never develop a sound preaching ministry that effectively reaches children and youth. Thus Part I of this book sets forth a theological rationale for the sermons and stories that follow in Part II. Part II illustrates my theological-creative methodology and gives a sampling of the approaches I have found most effective in my own Gospel-telling to children in grades one through six. The reader will soon discover that, although sound principles are indifferent to age (good preaching is good preaching because it proclaims, judges, recreates, and grounds us in God and his Kingdom), there are particular issues that arise whenever we address children.

I happen to believe that churches are showing renewed interest in inclusive worship: local churches are showing more concern about the participation of all ages in corporate worship. But I am less certain that pastors are showing that same concern when they prepare their children's sermons. Thus this handbook may serve the additional purpose of pricking the consciences of those of us—both clergy and lay people—who have paid shamefully little attention to the way in which we communicate the Gospel to children. How often have we waited until the last minute and then hurriedly paged through a book or racked our brains for a suitable tidbit to offer our small ones!

We have heard many rationalizations for deluding ourselves that a weekly children's sermon does not actually change lives, but theologically we know that nothing could be more important than sowing the seeds of the Gospel early in life. We tell ourselves that children don't listen, that they aren't mature enough to plumb the depths of the written Word, and that their time would be better spent in a Sunday school classroom.

Our excuses are endless and scarcely differ from the rationalizations we use to pass over the ineffectiveness of our adult sermons.

There must be an adage that sums up this problem, but since I couldn't find one, I wrote my own:

> *If we cannot reach children*
> *with God's great love,*
> *What hope is there for hearts and minds*
> *iced over with age?*

I repeat, then, my hope that this handbook will stimulate more than it will settle matters, and that it will make us more willing and more capable of communicating the Love that has found us.

As I mature in my own faith, I recognize and give thanks for the special people in my life who have shared the Gospel out of their rich imagination and dauntless enthusiasm. In addition, I would like to specifically thank two people for their contributions, insights, and suggestions: Professor Donald H. Graves, for his particular sensitivities and expertise in communicating with children; and the Reverend S. Russell Block, for his long-standing interest in proclaiming the Good News to children. And for their particular attention to details of all kinds, I am grateful to Priscilla Phenix and my wife, Ruth.

PART I

Laying A Firm Foundation

INTRODUCTION

In preparing this book I had one question uppermost in my mind: what constitutes effective communication with children? The question, of course, cuts across many different areas of the church's ministry to children. For example, anyone concerned about Christian education will also be interested in the art of Gospel-telling. Nevertheless, I have primarily limited myself to examining and explicating the communication of the Gospel within the context of worship. In this regard I have assumed that we want our children to be active participants in the liturgical life of the congregation. (Perhaps I have presumed too much, because not all churches feel strongly about including children in corporate worship. And, sad to say, some parents are quite upset if their children are not in Sunday school classes while they worship.) Although this book is not an explicit apologetic for a distinctive preaching ministry, the reader will recognize my belief in its validity.

Many justifications exist for an appropriate place and time for both worship and education, and for a natural flow between the two. Children should have the opportunity to experience worship which is both appropriate to their age and truly corporate (the entire congregation gathered) in places where the Gospel is always proclaimed. Children need a worship service which is appropriate to their age because their concerns, their level of understanding, and their interests are special. When they are the primary participants, worship can be a less formal, more spontaneous experience; we can tell the community's faith story in ways that speak their particular language. But children also need to be part of the church's corporate worship, in which we are bound together as one body and can sense the mystery and sacredness of being in God's presence. One might even argue that children belong at the Sunday service rather than in Sunday school classes, because this is the primary place where they are engaged in the pilgrimage of faith.[1]

Practically speaking, the Community Church of Durham has an age-appropriate chapel service the first and third Sundays of each month, and includes the children in the first part of its corporate worship on the other Sundays. During corporate worship, and especially during the chapel services, we actively engage the children and young people through direct participation and leadership roles. A full hour of Christian education follows, part of an educational program which is broken into trimesters, with three Celebration Sundays that include the entire congregation. Many other alternatives are also satisfactory,[2] provided they meet both kinds of worship needs.

We include children in corporate worship not so much for their sake as for the function they serve: they are a visible reminder that the Church is incomplete without them. Their presence enables us to realize more fully the childlike character of the Kingdom. Without their incorporation we might lose those special childlike qualities in our public worship: being joyful and spontaneous, pragmatic and expedient, understand-

[1]Notably, John H. Westerhoff, *Bringing up Children in the Christian Faith* (Minneapolis: Winston Press, 1980).

[2]In *A New Look for Sunday Morning* (Nashville: Abingdon, 1975), William B. Abernethy explores a congregation's effort to interweave worship, religious education, and celebration into a regular three-part Sunday morning experience. In *Children in the Worshipping Community* (Atlanta: John Knox Press, 1981), David Ng and Virginia Thomas argue *against* children's sermons or a special time for children within the worship service and argue *for* an integrated worship service. They are perfectly correct when they say that "worship can have the depth of content and the integrity that reflect the highest biblical and traditional standards and at the same time have appeal to children" (p. 24). On the other hand, they are presupposing the ideal situation, and never grapple with the negative aspects of having children present for the entire worship service. Obviously, we are not faced with an either-or situation but a "both-and" situation. I hope this book will convince its readers that preaching to and with children has an integrity of its own.

able and simple, universal and inclusive, stimulating and creative.

An effective children's sermon has much in common with a powerful adult sermon, yet it is different in important ways, too. Both the similarities and the differences, I trust, will become clearer as we proceed. In working through the material for this book, I became aware of how sloppily we use certain words and phrases, especially those that have recently been added to our homiletical vocabulary. At the beginning of Part II the reader will find a glossary of some of these terms, and at the end of Part I a decalogue of "Do's" for preparing children's sermons. I've tried not to take anything basic for granted, yet I know full well that more could be said about each of the issues raised in this section. I also sense that I have not lived up to my own high expectations in Part II, in which I offer samples of my own Gospel-telling to children. But what would goals be if they did not raise our expectations and give us something for which to aim?

TELLING THE OLD, OLD STORY—
IT'S NOT ALL THAT EASY

A good children's sermon is simple, direct, dramatic, and participatory; it has a single purpose, and enables the listener to experience God's story as his own. A poor children's sermon is dull, rambling, uncreative, overly verbal, and moralistic; it tries to teach too much, and gets stuck either in the past or the present.

The Trouble with Familiar Favorites

The typical children's homily attempts to tell a familiar biblical narrative in an interesting way. The underlying assumption is that children will assimilate the Christian faith in some mysterious way if they become acquainted with the major biblical events. But a number of dangers lurk in this approach. Children may be told about Adam and Eve, Noah and his ark, the crossing at the Red Sea (the Sea of Reeds), Jonah and the whale (the great fish), David and Goliath, Zacchaeus, and the Good Samaritan, but they are frequently left to devise their own interpretations of these stories. Children do internalize these accounts, but often with horrendous results.

Telling the Adam-and-Eve narrative as a literal story, for example, may result in banishing sin to some faraway time, localizing it to an unknown place, associating it with picking forbidden fruit, or confirming the cultural bias that snakes and women are not to be trusted. If we abide by a literal interpretation, we must be doubly cautious not to say anything that would encourage children's natural inclination to understand this story as another fairy tale. After all, it did happen a long time ago in a faraway place, and it did involve a talking snake and a man and a woman of universal significance. Our real obligation is to teach children that sin is what happens in backyards and playgrounds. The inevitability of sin as we presently experience it is the bridge which allows us to see how our own story is connected with the biblical story of the Fall.

If one is less concerned with the historical authenticity of Adam and Eve, then he faces a different set of problems. In this instance the minister or teacher must beware of implying anything that would later require children to relearn concepts when they study evolution. One of my cardinal rules is (whenever possible) to avoid teaching anything that will later lead to confusion. Of course it is not easy to explain to children how sin became woven into the very fabric of the evolutionary process, but more often than not the story is told literally, perhaps in updated form, and given a non-literal interpretation. In such a situation, the youngster must figure out a way to reconcile a fairy tale-like story with the reason why he put chewing gum on his teacher's chair.

We must remember that the biblical stories were not told and retold because of their historical content or scientific explanation; they remained alive and vital because they gave an identity to the people who passed them on. The story of Adam and Eve was told by a people who had already experienced sin and understood it to be disobedience against a God who had called them out of an existence marred by it. Their experience was specific and historical, but they also realized its universal nature. The result was a story which confirmed their history as a people who both entered into and broke the sacred covenant; it was more this kind of story than one that fully explained the historical or psychological origins of sin (though it may have done this in a way and to an extent that we as historians can no longer determine). Thus our own personal approach to this familiar favorite might help us to understand the difficulty of explaining the *origin* of sin and to emphasize instead our own history as individuals and members of a community which is filled with both promise *and* judgment.

6

As children we delighted in the intriguing stories of Noah's ark and Jonah and the whale, but we were left in the dark about their real significance. Our earliest fantasies abounded with animals marching two by two and mental pictures of what it would be like to live in the belly of a whale. But as our minds grew more logical, we puzzled over how Noah distinguished a male turtle from a female turtle, and how Jonah found sufficient oxygen to breathe. The situation is only aggravated by today's added confusions: children watch Yogi Bear's flying ark on T.V., and read about Pinocchio, who is swallowed by a whale during his misadventures.

We reason that immature minds cannot grasp the subtleties of stories written for adults, and content ourselves with telling children the details of biblical events. But if we wait to communicate their significance, we wait too long, and we must live with the consequences of our own mental laziness. Children become adults faster than we think, and if we put off explaining to them the true point of the story of Noah, there is a good chance that they will grow up imagining that the story's central message is about the miraculous power of a man to build a gigantic ark and survive forty days of rain with a menagerie of animals. We must remember that it is not so difficult for children to understand the childlike faith of a man who did not demand to have all the answers, to understand the necessity of starting over again when everything has gone wrong. They have the capacity to realize that the Hebrews preserved the story of Jonah not as a fairy tale, but as a story that shows how God's great mercy overwhelms our expectations and hopes for it. Certainly this isn't a message for adults only.

Storytellers, beware! Those very features that make a story interesting and arresting also divert us, clouding the life-and-death meaning they were originally meant to dramatize (cf Jesus' warning about signs versus *the* sign in Matthew 16:1-4).

The Misuse of Biblical Heroes

It is curious that Zacchaeus has been singled out among the many New Testament figures to be popularized. Like Johnny

Appleseed, he has become a natural part of childhood memories because of a catchy song, colorful pictures, and the ease with which we may play his role. My hunch is that Zacchaeus has become an all-time favorite because children can identify with the feeling of being small and disliked. (Just try having them identify with "the woman with a flow of blood" or one of the several lepers.) Children—especially boys—identify with David the giant-killer for similar reasons. Though not very old or very big, David put the bully in his place.

But herein lies the danger. With our help, children get carried away with the image of the little man in a sycamore tree or the boy with a slingshot. (What better justification for having their very own weapons of destruction?) As a result, all of the shock, dismay, and offense of the narrative is lost, as is the conclusion. It was nice that Jesus invited himself to Zacchaeus' house for dinner; but it was also scandalous because Zacchaeus was a rich, powerful tax collector who was despised by his own blood brothers. His turnabout (conversion) is comprehensible only as we see the manner in which God invites the weakest, loneliest, and most scorned to be his guests in the fellowship of his Kingdom, and only as we see *that they accept.* King David represents the other side of the coin. In his rise to glory and power, we see someone who is loved by all and thereby falls in love with himself. In this instance salvation is accomplished when the man who has everything loses all that is dear to him in order that God may continue to use him. As teachers and ministers, we would be foolish if we did not build upon the fact that children can identify with characters like David and Zacchaeus, but we should not lose the Good News among sycamore trees and slingshots.

Very little irritates me more than the annual massacre of the story of the Good Samaritan. He has become the paradigm of virtue because he stopped to help one in need as others passed by. But do children realize that the irony lies in the fact that the Samaritan was a half-breed, both racially and religiously? This story was not considered gospel because it had a moralistic point. The parable is Jesus' answer to the question about the limits of love (Who can be called my neighbor?). In the echo story included in this handbook, you will find the usual emphasis on helping someone who is hurting, but you will also find a frequently omitted "hook": that the Good Samaritan is a member of a motorcycle gang. Children perceive this as a contradiction, yet it is this very contradiction that gives the story its impact and carries its radical message. Although this may seem like a minor point, it makes a difference between a sentimental story of a do-gooder, and a shocking account demonstrating that even a half-breed can show the unlimited quality of Christian love.

It was a group of city-toughened nine and ten-year-olds who helped me understand that the command to love becomes radicalized only when we acknowledge the personal risk involved in stopping to help someone lying alongside a notoriously dangerous side road. As we were discussing the story of the Good Samaritan, I asked them whether they would stop to help someone lying in a gutter. "No way" was their response. The person might be a thief playing a trick or a "mad" drunk with a broken bottle under his coat, they explained. We as adults might more clearly see the difference between simply "being good" and discipleship if the situation involved stopping our car to see if a person lying by the side of the road needed help. Like the priest and the Levite, we would consider all the reasons why we *should not* stop, and by then we would have driven too far to consider turning around. And, like us, children tend to adopt "safe" interpretations of this parable of radical love: being a Good Samaritan becomes helping little old ladies across the street.

The Confusion of Love and Law

The Sermon on the Mount is another favorite choice of hurried ministers or reluctant Sunday school teachers in search of a quick lesson. Most children have been taught Jesus' dictum about turning the other cheek, and they usually interpret it as an invitation to cowardliness. Parents are often equally confused, because on the one hand they want their child to obey Jesus' commandment, and on the other hand they are fearful that their good intentions will lead their son or daughter to be bullied. Matthew 5:39 thus offers a prime example of what happens when a passage is isolated and transposed *in toto* into a child's world. If a young boy builds his ego with his physical prowess, it is very likely that he will confuse humility with timidity, and vicarious suffering with being a doormat. This section of the Sermon on the Mount is indeed the core of Jesus' ethic (Rom. 12:14ff.), but it cannot be so simply reduced to a single charge. And children are not too young to begin to understand that it takes greater strength to practice love than hate, greater power to walk away from a fight than to start one (see "Show Me How Strong You Are" and "Giving Love a Chance"). But they can only begin to understand this if they begin to see that Jesus did not come to give us new laws but to empower us to love as we never have before.

We may also be guilty of practicing a double standard, and thereby may teach what we do not intend to teach through our "adult" behavior. We may be quick to expect our own child to bravely walk away from a fight, but as parents we may reject as overly idealistic, or stupid, the injunction to give our overcoat to someone who has just sued us for our coat (Matt. 5:40). When we take seriously the radical nature of the Gospel (its good news and its implications), we cannot miss the folly of trying to be Christ-like in our behavior without first having given our lives to Christ so that he may live within us (I Cor. 1:23; Gal. 2:20). And whenever we minimize the Gospel—whether by turning it into law(s) or by cheapening its demand—*we delude ourselves into thinking that the Kingdom can be built with willpower.*

Two Prescriptions for Improvement

Whenever we believe it is easy or sufficient to tell the old, old story, we should employ two helpful guidelines. The first is to begin with the day-to-day experience of the children to whom we are talking (see, for example, "Breakfast of Champions"). Elementary-school children in America are so competitive that it is almost frightening, but it is a fact of life; thus we should begin with this assumption and proceed to demonstrate that "there is a better way" (I Cor. 12:31b).

The second guideline is to assume that most of the Bible was written by adults for adults—something that should make us wary of literal applications and transposition of almost any biblical text. A graphic reminder is the Sunday school teacher who sat stoically telling her class how the men of Gibeah ravished the Levite's concubine and then cut her into pieces and "mailed" the parts all over the countryside (it's in the Bible, after all). But equally disastrous is concluding that adult themes cannot be translated for children. We get ourselves into trouble when we mistake the context for the message, as the Sunday school teacher did, or when we confuse the simplicity of the Gospel with the complexity of its application. None of us knowingly neglects the importance of building a sound spiritual foundation for children, but clearly we have been guilty of offering them the husk instead of the kernel of faith.

PREACHING A GOOD
CHILDREN'S SERMON

Preparing Carefully

Dr. Paul Scherer of Union and Princeton Theological Seminaries gave his homiletical students this rule of thumb: for every minute in the pulpit, spend one hour in preparation. If we ministers tend to short-cut the "main feature" with a Saturday-night special, we are even more inclined to hope that the Holy Spirit will do our work for us when we prepare a children's message. Yet our better sense tells us that the children's sermon is just as important, minute for minute, as the adult sermon.

How often have we heard a parishioner say, "You know, I get more out of the children's stories than the adult sermons." We are keenly aware that what we say in those few minutes extends beyond "little ears," and I suspect one reason is that everyone likes to listen in. This suggests—and not always so subtly—that too many parishioners lose the central thrust of what we are saying when we take twenty minutes to say it. If the children's message is the "best part," then perhaps it deserves more attention than it usually receives. The answer is neither to make our adult sermons more childish nor to create children's messages that are more sophisticated, but to make both more "portable."

Integrating the Sermon into Worship—and Life

The children's sermon should not be isolated and obtrusive. Every service of corporate worship should be planned around a central theme, and the children's homily should represent a development of that theme for a particular age level. When the children's sermon is not part of a general theme, even the most well thought-out message only reinforces the assumption that it is a nice sidelight that is occasionally included. I think it is much more difficult to develop a good message when we have unlimited freedom: if we try to develop a great idea or a creative gimmick of our choice, we often find our wheels spinning. In short, the Scripture text that is the basis for the adult sermon should also be the foundation of the children's sermon—for practical as well as theological reasons.

But the children's sermon should be related to more than the immediate context of the Sunday worship service. The minister should also be aware of the subject matter being studied in Sunday school. The Uniform or International Lesson Plan has the distinct advantage of allowing everyone in a congregation to share in a continuous way the same learning experience. (The original purpose of the International Lesson Plan, which was developed in 1872, has remained unchanged: little Baptist boys in Burma and adult Methodists in Minnesota would be studying the identical printed questions on the same Sunday. See *The Big Little School*, mentioned in the bibliography. Unfortunately, the newer curriculums do not make the minister's task easy: he must invariably choose between following the lectionary or the Sunday-school curriculum, or find the time to integrate the two. Yet simply being aware of the curriculum enables the pastor to avoid a total separation between Sunday worship and Sunday-school teaching. At the very least, he should not be guilty of presenting a children's sermon that has nothing to do with the basic message of the worship service that morning. And ideally the minister should be preaching and teaching to both children and adults with a sense of where he is leading the congregation over an extended period of time.[3]

At some time in his ministry, every pastor feels frustrated and pessimistic about the power of the spoken word to change

[3]For an extended discussion of sermon-planning that leads the congregation, see Richard J. Coleman, "What Aggravates Me About the Preaching I Hear," *The Pulpit*, December 1968.

a person's life, and he critiques his messages to adults. We need to ask ourselves the same critical questions about our preaching/teaching ministry to children. Is it making a difference? The question deserves much greater consideration than we can give it here, but I want to stress one important point: that reinforcement is imperative to the learning process. The minister/teacher is naive if he does not admit that children are just as likely as adults to let a sermon go in one ear and out the other —although children do have a way of listening when they appear to be inattentive, just as adults have a way of appearing to be listening when they are actually woolgathering.

Thus we are responsible for continually searching out methods to reinforce the Gospel's message. With a few exceptions (such as the home church), the process through which the spoken word modifies behavior happens away from the sanctuary, either at home or in school, but especially in peer groups. Again, the necessity of careful planning cannot be over-emphasized; if it is ignored, the children's sermon, like the adult sermon, will wither and die in its location. The minister can make use of the adults listening in, and even at times address them personally, to ask their help in reinforcing the message.

The sermon "My One-Tenth Box" is an example of learning that begins in the sanctuary but is meant to be continued as a family pattern at home. This handbook also offers several stories and demonstrations that are purposefully left unfinished, because they are meant to be discussed, extended, and completed at home (e.g., "Fifty-two Card Pick-up" and "A Prince in Disguise"). Although I haven't included a serial, it is possible to begin one and let it continue for several weeks, so long as each part of it makes an independent point. The minister as preacher should not be embarrassed about repeating a particular theme, especially when it lays bare the heart of the Gospel. (See the sermons focused on what it means to be a prophet or the theme of love overcoming hate, which is developed from several perspectives.)

Supporting One Central Point

Dr. Paul Scherer also emphasized the value of being sure that each sermon has one central point, and that everything flows toward or away from that point. He asked the students submitting sermons to him to accompany each one with a cover page that included a one-sentence summary of the message. And we should apply the same method to our children's sermons. Of course, we are always tempted to make a number of worthwhile observations, especially when we have hit upon a creative idea. But overusing object lessons often results in a stringing-together of numerous little points which in the end obscure the central point.

In the sermon "All the Glue in the World," one child is invited to destroy a beautiful flower while another child is challenged to restore it to its original beauty. Because this sermon raises several important issues—good stewardship, the sacredness of life, a subtle proof of God's existence—it is tempting to mention all three truths, particularly because the drama cannot be repeated. The alternative is to carefully construct the proclamation so that it can be effective at more than one level. Instead of indulging in overkill, or using an approach that forces everyone to follow a strictly logical path, construct the sermon (situation) so that older children and adults can intuitively perceive a certain richness which they can pursue later.

As part of my own discipline and by way of example, I have included a one-sentence summary of each sermon in this handbook. But bear in mind that a summary and a conclusion are not identical. Conclusions must sometimes be played by ear, but summaries—those central points—should always be clarified ahead of time. Only after you outline a sermon can you examine it for unity, weed out what is extraneous and distracting, and sharpen its primary purpose. Although most of us do not write out children's sermons, we lose a great deal if we do not write down a summary statement and fill in a basic outline.

Encouraging Participatory Communication

In the last decade much has been written about media being the message. Not only are we more conscious of communication techniques themselves, but we are better prepared to evaluate the effectiveness of whatever media resources we employ. After a flurry of interest in such techniques as dialogue sermons, closed-circuit T.V., feedback sessions, audio-visual shows, chancel drama, and multi-media effects, ministers and Christian educators have settled for a more balanced approach to communication. It is certainly true that preaching still relies too heavily upon a one-way verbal process, something that is especially true when children are the primary audience, because their verbal skills are not highly developed. But both experts and non-experts agree on the importance of involving the listener, regardless of her age. Involvement includes not only engaging the five senses (and perhaps too much stock has been put into flashy, expensive multimedia effects which attempt to stimulate these senses), but also engaging the mind and the body in such a way that the listener feels *she* is on the verge of making an important decision for *her* life.

In training prospective teachers, instructors often use a "learning pyramid" to demonstrate the relative values of three different methods of communication.[4]

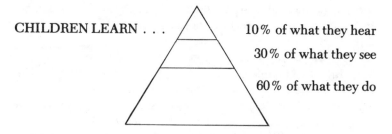

CHILDREN LEARN . . .

10% of what they hear

30% of what they see

60% of what they do

We know from practical experience that the greater an individual's involvement in a learning situation, the greater the chances that he will retain what he has learned. For example, the reader is more likely to remember the information just presented if he receives the visual stimulus of the pyramid rather than the verbal stimulus of a long descriptive paragraph. Similarly, learning to ride a bicycle is usually a lasting

[4]If the reader wishes to pursue learning theory as it relates to religious development and change, I recommend Thomas Groome, *Christian Religious Education: Sharing Our Story and Vision* (San Francisco: Harper & Row, 1980); and James E. Loder, *The Transforming Moment: Understanding Convictional Experiences* (San Francisco: Harper & Row, 1981).

learning experience because it demands the total participation of the individual who is learning.

Because of the nature of their development, their span of concentration, and their exposure to mass media, children have a built-in screen against excessive verbal communication. In their early years they learn through seeing, touching, tasting, and feeling. Consequently, most ministers have learned the value of arming themselves with "props" when they tell a children's sermon. They make the abstract concrete and provide important visual clues for the message. But props do not necessarily assure the success of a children's sermon; they can also divert the children's attention and obscure the central point. Thus the ministers armed with objects should not automatically assume that they will reach the apex of the communication process with children. In fact, we never reach the apex, although we get much closer to it when our sermons follow the pattern of learning to ride a bike.

The Broadway hit musical *Godspell* is such a delight because it presents biblical material (parables, sayings, narrative, and action) in fresh and diverse ways. I selected the sermons in this handbook because they also suggest a variety of ways to preach the Gospel other than the usual stand-up monologue delivered with an object in hand. For obvious reasons the emphasis is on methods of non-verbal communication. As ministers and teachers of children, we have the distinct advantage of knowing immediately how effective we are. If hands and feet begin to fidget, and heads begin to turn and mouths to open, then we know we have lost them. I was once surprised during a children's sermon I was giving when a boy of seven flashed me a particular sign we had learned in Vacation Bible School two weeks earlier (the thumb pointed horizontally and the index finger pointing vertically). At the time I was wondering if any of the eighty restless children were hearing me. If one child had, then I had reason to hope that others had also identified with the non-verbal sign which gave them a special sense of identity as Christians.

Most congregations are filled with resources that most certainly should be tapped. Among the members are artists, musicians, engineers, and actors who are usually happy to be asked to assist in a special project. In a Presbyterian church in New Jersey, for example, a high-school shop teacher had put together a working robot which the minister used effectively in a number of children's sermons. Although such creativity is a great thing, we must also make sure that it never displaces the Gospel message itself.

Participatory communication requires that we try to forego using notes during the presentation. Notes not only spoil the sense of spontaneity, but also keep us from freely using our hands. Body movements—those non-verbal signs of communication—are always important, and children are keenly aware of their significance. Spontaneity and involvement, of course, are never a substitute for careful preparation, because without the latter the sermon is sure to ramble and lose its focus.

Targeting the Sermon

Unfortunately, on most Sundays the minister sees before him a group of children ranging from toddlers to adolescents. Ideally, he would like to have a small group of preschoolers or children of elementary-school or junior-high age. But since the ideal is usually impossible, the minister should at least be aware of some basic differences in the ways in which these age groups perceive and verbalize reality. As a general rule, the pastor should aim his sermon at the lowest common denominator, which would normally be first to second grade. But because it naturally takes more effort to enter into a child's world and adopt a child's way of expressing things, ministers too often address older children, because they are closer to this age group in mental and verbal abilities. The negative result is a poor excuse for a children's sermon: an adult sermon reduced to pint size.

Preschoolers. The most important rule to remember is that preschoolers are not capable of understanding abstractions or thinking symbolically. Words are not so much a symbol of some reality as a coequal representation of some specific reality. Attributes like "red," "big," "fast," and "good" are embodied in the person or object itself. "Dog" is Spot down the street rather than all dogs in the world. Preschoolers may come to understand the cross as the thing on which Jesus died, but they will not comprehend the Cross as a symbol of Christ's death for humanity. Consequently, teachers of the Word should watch the use of metaphors, allegories, and even parables. On the other hand, children of this age love role-playing, let's-pretend games, rhymes, magic, riddles, and stories that are not allegorical (see, for example, "Stilling the Storm," "The Story of Tom Gobble," and "Death Comes to the Henry Family").

The second fact to remember is that preschoolers think in literal terms. They do not clearly distinguish between fantasy and reality. These limitations mean that children sometimes draw unusual conclusions from what they hear and see. The first time I told the story "Looking for the Devil," my own child alerted me to the necessity of watching my language. In trying to make the point that evil is not really a red character with a pitchfork tail who makes us do bad things, I had innocently said, "The Devil is inside you." Several weeks later my four-year-old daughter asked me one night at supper, "Daddy, is there a Devil in my stomach?" By a process of literal association, she had come to the simple conclusion that if the Devil doesn't live somewhere outside here, then he must live inside her, and where else but in her stomach—a conclusion made "logical" by the fact that she had a stomachache. It is this predisposition toward literalism that also explains why preschoolers inevitably misinterpret analogies, although ministers persist in using them because they occur so frequently in the four Gospels. Biblical scholarship may have relieved us of this burden (if it is a burden of obligation) by demonstrating that most or all allegories were originally parables of participation that the Church turned into parables of illustration (see below, "The Story Form as Proclamation").

As adults we may find it strange that children do not share our fear of death—so strange that we continually try to protect them from seeing signs of death. How quickly we forget that children do not see reality and fantasy as two distinct realms. In their minds fact and fantasy are likely to be interchangeable, which explains why biblical miracles are neither puzzling nor awe-inspiring to preschoolers. Although children of this age can move easily and literally in either realm, the minister/teacher should not view this perceptual stage as a stumbling block. Instead, he should accept it as an invitation to vary his presentations with let's-pretend stories and role-playing. Every minister's library should not be without one sound-effects record; with it he can transform any context into "the real thing." One of the sermons in this collection, "Stilling the Storm," gives children many opportunities to sense and feel what it is like to be in a small boat in a big sea, and they will have no difficulty believing they are really there. It is too bad that more adults aren't capable of this kind of "teleportation."

Elementary-School Children.   After a child enters school, he changes markedly. Among the most important changes is his need to demonstrate both to his peers and to himself that he belongs and that he is capable of being independent. By age eight or nine, his center of gravity begins to shift from home to school by "hanging around with the gang." Parents are often distressed by what their child is learning through his peer group, and say so. As a result, the minister only underscores this disapproval when he writes sermons in which morality is codified in do's and don't's, and in which the virtue of being a Christian is presented as being different or standing alone. By far the most realistic situations are ones in which elementary-school children are conscious of peer interaction (see "What to Do with a Chocolate Chip Cookie?"), or in which children of the same age act out their real-life tensions (see "Show Me How Strong You Are"). Most effective is communication that flows in and through the group, in contrast to communication which flows from the minister/teacher to the children.

The older elementary-school child is much more interested in mastering and controlling reality.[5] She is both able and eager to distinguish clearly between reality and fantasy. Magic becomes fascinating to her because, just as she has figured out some basic rules about the universe, someone comes along and seems to defy them. At the same time she is less interested in the world of fantasy and more likely to identify with the real people of adventure stories: Princess Leia of *Star Wars* or Carolyn Ingalls of *Little House on the Prairie* (rather than Snow White or Little Red Riding Hood) are liable to be her heroines because she can consider emulating them. As she grows older, historical or contemporary figures of great achievement tend to displace these super-heroes. "Let's-pretend" now seems childish because the youngster wants a real challenge, but role-playing is still acceptable if the roles are realistic. In fact, role-playing can be valuable if it gives the older child an opportunity to experiment with what it will be like to be older.

Despite these changes, children this age have a limited perception of time—and the teacher in each of us becomes anxious when children cannot separate Old Testament stories from New Testament stories. Often our best efforts are frustrated when a child makes Moses and Jesus contemporaries. What we must remember is that, to preschoolers, time is nothing more than a patchwork of uncoordinated events. Even during the middle years of childhood, time is limited to the narrow span between the ages of baby brother and grandma. It is only when children are far along in elementary school or in early adolescence that they can put into perspective two thousand years of biblical history and nineteen hundred years of church history. Thus we might as well wait until then to worry about untangling the prophet Isaiah from the apostle Paul, and concentrate instead on what a prophet or a disciple *is*. Do not misunderstand me—there is no harm in doing what

[5]There are, of course, more definite classifications of religious development. Lawrence Kohlberg, for example, has identified six states occurring at three distinct levels: pre-conventional, conventional, and post-conventional. For a discussion of Kohlberg's theory of moral development, see *Moral Development: A Guide to Piaget and Kohlberg* by Ronald Duska and Mariellen Whelan (New York: Paulist Press, 1975).

21

we can to lay a foundation for a framework of time. But we must remember that there is a "ripe" time to teach the chronological facts of our heritage. Still, we should not wait until children are able to sort out the morass of historical events before we begin to instill in them God's concern for his creation as it unfolds in time and historical events.

Watching Your Language

No matter what the age group, watch your language. Some ministers and teachers seem either to talk as if their audience were crossword addicts, or to choose words carelessly. My advice is to take nothing for granted. A simple explanation of a key word is one way of getting into your theme. (See "A Prince in Disguise," in which the word "disguise" is first explained.) Ministers are prone to overlook the fact that children do not live in a biblical world and therefore have a limited understanding of words like "reconciliation," "righteousness," "repentance," "salvation," "covenant," "apostle," "grace," "sin," and "holy." We should not use words of this kind unless we clarify them first.

We all know at least one humorous story about a child who misunderstood a word and came up with an unheard-of interpretation of it. I once referred to Jesus as being of the house and lineage of David. Realizing that I probably was not being understood, I added, to explain myself, that Jesus was a descendant of King David. Later, a girl approached me hesitantly and said as politely as she could, "Mr. Coleman, I'm sure glad Jesus descended from David and not into Hell."

Often we unwittingly choose words that reflect a dualism we do not intend; for example, we may casually refer to "God up there" or "the Devil down there." Since children can learn as much from our mistakes as from our good intentions, we must beware—particularly of the more insidious form of dualism that invites children to participate in the sacred and the spiritual on Sunday but live in the real world of the secular and material during the week. We undermine Christian faith when we find ourselves using a distinct biblical language to convey what was originally proclaimed in the vernacular. Rather than talking about sin as a doctrine or a concept, why not explain sin as children experience it and give it a name afterward? I have not yet met a child who knew what it meant when he was told that Jesus died for his sins. "What does Jesus have to do with sin, whatever that is?" he wonders. More than two thousand years separate a middle-class American and a Jewish Messiah, and repeating the well-worn phrases will not build any bridges. We need to forget about even attempting to translate those short-hand symbols we learned to decode only after a college degree and several years of theological training. If, instead, we use those experiences that bind all of us humans together, we will discover that we all speak the same language.

Developing Your Tone

Placed in a larger context, watching our language is part of watching ourselves. To a very significant extent the medium is the message, and in this instance the minister is the primary medium. A most revealing exercise is asking a friend to observe you. One Sunday have him block out your voice in order to be more sensitive to other stimuli; the next Sunday have him block out all visual stimuli in order to acutely observe the verbal quality of your sermon. In this way your observer will develop a good sense of both the verbal and nonverbal situation *you are creating*. The result will help you start the process of examining the tone of your Gospel-telling.

Tone has to do with more than just delivery. Ultimately, it raises questions concerning identity: *who you are* (how do you feel about yourself? how do you project yourself?) *who you are in relationship to your audience* (you are big, and they are small; you know it all, so they must learn from you; you are very much like them, yet very different; you are the father, and they are your children); and *who you are together* (they are the exposed ones sitting in front; we are the ones having a private conversation; we are the ones sharing stories about God and his people).

Because questions of identity are involved, most of us feel that we can't do much to change the tonal quality of our presence. You may think of yourself as a "natural" with children, or you may feel awkward with them. Regardless of the validity of such a generalization, you can change a great deal once you

23

begin paying attention to the situation you create by the little things you do or don't do.

To a certain extent you will be limited by the particular physical circumstances of your corporate worship, but reassess these factors: they are important, but not overriding. To shape the more immediate context of you and your listeners, start by asking what you want to communicate about yourself and this special time with the children of your church. It will then be possible for you to affect such factors as physical distance (standing or sitting, at the same level or at a higher level), your dress (do you always wear a robe?), the quality of your voice, your use of questions (rhetorical questions, discussion starters, etc.), and your use of physical contact (do you and the children ever touch?). The less time you have—and usually you don't have very much—the more these factors are heightened. Thus, even your opening sentence becomes critical. As all of these impressions unite, you communicate a certain tonal quality. You will create the atmosphere by the kind of communication you choose: celebration, proclamation, explanation, dialogue, or lecture. And children will either perceive the sermon as "their time" or "your time"; they will sense whether you are preaching *at* them or sharing *with* them.

Tone is important whenever we communicate, but it is even more important when we communicate with children. The content of a message may prove to be irrelevant, untimely, or aimed at an age level different from that of the group we are addressing. But children almost always pick up the tone of the message. Various studies have demonstrated that children are particularly influenced by their assessment of the speaker's intentions and the meaning of the situation.[6] Since younger children are less confident about the use of language, they give more weight to nonlinguistic clues, which they understand better. This factor can work both to our advantage and our disadvantage. On the one hand, we need not despair if children miss the central point of a message; the tone of a sermon may succeed when the content fails.

"Baa-Baa," for example, is a story (in this handbook)

[6]Margaret Donaldson, *Children's Minds* (New York: W. W. Norton & Company, 1978), Chapter 6.

about the loving concern of God, which searches us out when we have gone astray. The story as it unfolds relies upon an allegory of a lamb named Baa-Baa who gets lost, and a good shepherd who leaves the flock in order to find him. Before I told the story I had hoped that the older preschoolers would catch the analogy. But, as I should have anticipated, they could not make the connection between the good shepherd and God. Nevertheless, they were touched by the tone of the story, by the shepherd's caring and the lamb's great worth. So at one level the sermon missed the mark, but on a tonal level it succeeded. A similar example is the sermon "Death Comes to the Henry Family," because some of its concepts about life after death may be too abstract for younger minds. Nevertheless, the emotive qualities of assurance and anticipation can be easily translated into nonverbal clues that children can understand.

But children's limited linguistic skills also create dangers. The art of Gospel-telling inevitably encourages the use of picturesque speech (similes, metaphors, mental images, etc.), and the tone of a sermon is more likely to be carried by these kinds of language forms than by content-laden words. Once the minister/teacher has sparked a child's imagination, it may, of course, continue to run while the human voice drones on. But the consequences of this can be as disastrous as they are valuable. The stimulus of the language may set the stage for further thought, but it might also trigger associations which are not helpful. Truly disastrous is the child's receiving a conflicting message: one from the content and another from the tone of the sermon. In this situation he does not know which is the intended message, and so tends to ignore both.

Using Scripture Appropriately

How does the minister/teacher let children know that his message is not his own but God's as recorded in Scripture? I personally find it too artificial and ritualistic to always begin or end with a reading of Scripture. If a children's sermon ends up being humanistic or moralistic, attaching a biblical text will not redeem it. On the other hand, a sermon that is thoroughly biblical in its content and purpose but says nothing about its origin and motivation runs the risk of separating the

25

message from the Messenger. As ministers and teachers of the Word, we should do nothing to add to the misapprehension that many children already harbor—the mistaken idea that Noah's Ark is an original Walt Disney creation, the Ten Commandments a Paramount production, and the story of Johnny Appleseed an Old Testament story.

The issue is how to be explicit without being overly explicit. The sermons "A Prince in Disguise" and "What to Do with a Chocolate Chip Cookie?" illustrate the quandary in which we often find ourselves. Theologically speaking, neither one needs a biblical reference to validate it. Yet to omit the Prince's origin in Matthew's story of the Great Judgment in chapter twenty-five leaves the children in doubt about the story's model. But if the minister/teacher is overly explicit— that is, if he reads an appropriate Scriptural text about justice and hunger before he gives out one or two cookies—then he dissipates the degree of conflict which the sermon needs.

I am sure that we often find ourselves quoting Jesus as a kind of conclusion to our sermons. Or perhaps we depend upon a brief prayer or the context of worship to communicate the embodiment of God's love in all that we say and do. At times I find this satisfactory, and at other times I do not. But I do make it a rule that when I quote Scripture or repeat a saying of Jesus, I do so from a Bible in hand and not from notes or memory. My inclination is to treat each sermon individually but always with an eye toward demonstrating the Gospel as God's message.

Though we may be entirely certain where our inspiration comes from, it may not always be evident to the children who face us. Making this clear is an obligation we bear as ministers and teachers of the Word—a responsibility which demands our continual attention.

THE PURPOSE BEHIND
OUR PREACHING

Encouraging Ethical Development

Currently there is a great deal of interest in the progressive nature of human development. Jean Piaget and Erik Erikson were pioneers in this field, the former concentrating on conceptual development (especially that of children and adolescents), and the latter explaining human development by psycho-social stages. More recently, Gail Sheehy in *Passages* (1974) and Daniel J. Levinson in *The Seasons of a Man's Life* (1978) have directed our attention to the specific stages of adult life. In addition, Lawrence Kohlberg, building upon the work of Piaget, has worked out a theory of moral development; and Jim Fowler, following in the tradition of Piaget, Erikson, and Kohlberg, has mapped out the stages in the development of faith.[7]

The foundation of all these theories is the thesis that at various stages in our development there are certain determining patterns of operation that structure the content of our thinking and channel our emotional-psychic energies. These stages are *sequential* because there is an appropriate time for each developmental task to be learned, and *invariant* because one step necessarily follows another. In addition, these stages

[7]Jim Fowler and Sam Keen, *Life Maps: Conversations on the Journey to Faith* (Waco, Texas: Word Books, 1978). Besides discussing his own theory of faith commitment, Fowler discusses Kohlberg and provides a bibliography of his writings. Fowler has recently updated his research in *Stages of Faith: The Psychology of Human Development and the Quest for Meaning* (San Francisco: Harper & Row, 1981).

are *hierarchical* because each successive stage builds upon and carries forward in modified and augmented form the operations of the previous stage. Finally, researchers have tried to show that these stages are *universal*—that is, consistent from group to group and from culture to culture.

The question we ask is how this research might affect the pastor/teacher who prepares for Sunday morning. It clearly would be helpful if he had a summary knowledge of how we as humans develop physically, psychologically, morally, conceptually, and religiously. Such an understanding would help him develop reasonable expectations and assist him in targeting God's message. But I seriously doubt that the pastor/teacher needs in-depth knowledge of this subject. In the first place, it is false to assume that there is no value in a sermon that overshoots the particular developmental stage of the audience. As teachers/pastors we should be challenging the listener to understand his particular situation from a perspective that is one and sometimes two stages beyond his present stage of development. Although the listener does not need to know that we are purposely overshooting the mark, we ought to be aware that a specific sermon is working at more than one level. The key is to strike a balance between appealing to a level of maturity that is yet impossible and "talking down" to our audience in order to be sure that we are understood.

Secondly, we must remember that in faith the rational and the emotive are fused together. We can be overly concerned about mapping a child's progress in terms of certain coordinates, and so completely miss the fact that she has been unable to integrate knowing and doing, reason and will. Fowler is most instructive when he delineates the final two stages in the development of faith, in which cognition and commitment, motivation and action come together; in other words, the indicative (seeing what justice requires) and the imperative (doing what justice requires) are integrated.[8]

It seems that every good children's sermon aims at *demonstrating* what Christian faith is when it is acted upon. Naturally, the developmental stage of the audience will affect how a demonstration looks, and the kind of motivation it produces.

[8]Fowler and Keen, *Life Maps*, pp. 82ff.

Balancing Content and Motivation

It is entirely appropriate to ask whether there is a distinctive Christian content that is to be taught at an appropriate time. (The question also has serious consequences for Christian education and curriculum development.) Ronald Duska and Mariellen Whelan, authors of *Moral Development*, relate an incident which took place during a Christian-Marxist dialogue. The atheist-communist Herbert Aptheker was asked why he devoted himself so completely to his cause when he did not believe in God. "Aptheker smiled benignly, and in a calm, soft voice responded in words to this effect: 'Why? Because my cause is the service of my fellow man.' He then went on to remind the audience that this had been the great message of all organized religions."[9]

This incident reminds us that very often Christian morality looks like any other kind of morality, whether it is religious or atheistic or humanistic. Reinhold Niebuhr pointed out that there is no such thing as a Christian action, only Christians who perform Christ-like acts. And Dietrich Bonhoeffer warned that Christian faith must be distinguished from being religious in a particular way.[10] In different ways these philosophers and theologians are telling us that Christian proclamation not only raises questions about what one *should* do, but also provides the reasons and the *motivation* for those actions. Ministers who are preoccupied with religious development and moral behavior are also the most likely to be preoccupied with content to the extent that they neglect motivation and our very be-ing in Christ.

On the other hand, I am not willing to relinquish the distinctive character of the Christian content we communicate. For example, if someone is at a stage of religious development in which group relationships determine ideals, we are obligated to hold up the Church, a group of God's chosen people, as the primary group through which the individual learns

---

[9]Duska and Whelan, *Moral Development*, p. 81.

[10]Bonhoeffer expressed it well when he wrote: "It is not some religious act which makes a Christian what he is, but participation in the suffering of God in the life of the world" (letter dated July 18th, 1944, in *Letters and Papers from Prison*, ed. Eberhard Bethge [New York: Macmillan, 1953]).

about stewardship versus exploitation. Wouldn't we expect the belief statements of a community of faith to be different from that of a quasi-religious group which has collapsed the vertical into the horizontal? Kohlberg's understanding of the levels of moral development offers another illustration. As a child grows older (though age is only one factor), he moves through the first two stages of moral development (Level I, the pre-conventional level)—from a morality based upon anticipated punishment and reward to a concept of reciprocal fairness based upon a specific set of rules. Within this context we have two options: we can teach that the good is what God allows and the bad is what God forbids, and woe unto anyone if he does what God forbids; or we can teach that God wants every child to be happy (have life more abundantly), and certain rules will help him to be happy and fulfilled. (See Matthew 5:48, in which "fulfilled" might be a better translation for "perfect.") In this instance, choosing which approach to use to help a young child bring order to his life makes a crucial difference in the portrayal of God: in the first picture he is a tyrant; in the second, a friend. If our content implicitly teaches that "God will not like you if you do bad things," then we have only reinforced the pre-conventional level, at which only a narrow view of God is possible; we have done nothing to help the child move beyond a level where good and bad are judged solely upon their painful consequences.

I hope the reader will see that I do not want to separate good teaching from inspirational preaching. Whether we are communicating the Gospel to children or adults, both are necessary. My experience, however, has been that ministers facing a congregation of children overdo teaching to the detriment of proclamation. Perhaps I have already exposed a few of the faulty assumptions behind children's sermons that concentrate entirely upon teaching sound content, but undoubtedly the principal culprits are moralism and humanism.

Escaping Moralism and Humanism

The Trap of Moralism. Moralism is such an easy trap to fall into! Without constant vigilance it simply happens, because we do not have before us a clear-cut distinction between moralism and the Good News, between the indicative and the imperative. The indicative is the Good News that through Jesus Christ (his death and resurrection), each of us is invited into a new relationship with God. The imperative is the ethical response (both personal and social) that we make as the new creation begins to transform us. The imperative is grounded in the indicative, not vice versa. More than any other contemporary theologian, Rudolf Bultmann has insisted (e.g., in *Jesus & the Word*) that Jesus was not the bearer of a new ethic (rules of conduct), but the one who radicalizes the will of God by demanding an either/or decision to his invitation. While I would not go so far as to empty the Gospel of all of its specific Christian content, there can be no doubt that the Gospels portray the historical Jesus as being primarily concerned with confronting individuals with either/or decisions about their future relationship with God and their neighbors.

If the degeneration of children's sermons into insipid humanistic stories is the Church's primary problem in teaching children, its next-largest problem is confusing the Gospel with character-building. I suppose the confusion is partly due to ministers' efforts to make concrete the abstract doctrines about forgiveness and atonement. But from the child's point of view the Good News may seem to be nothing more than sermons about being more respectful, industrious, kind, honest, and positive, and less wasteful, cranky, temperamental, selfish, and mean. In the hierarchy of virtues, these would head almost every parent's list. Nevertheless, this approach unconsciously grounds the imperative in the indicative; in other words, it is cutting off the stem and expecting the flower to bloom. (An adult parallel would be trying to scare cigarette smokers into kicking their habit.) As ministers and teachers we make a serious mistake if we assume that children are only capable of understanding the Gospel in terms of do's and don't's. *The goal of every children's sermon should be the grounding of God's expectations of what we can be in the communication of God's love and acceptance of us as we are.*

Unfortunately, most children's sermons aim at adjusting children's behavior, instead of helping them develop a radically new way of looking at their relationship with God. The

31

negative consequence is that children experience love as law when they should be experiencing law as love; as Paul Scherer explains it, "Love experienced as Law ceases to be Love. Law experienced as Love ceases to be Law."[11] Practically speaking, this does not mean that every sermon should have as its sole purpose the conversion of the child. But it does mean that every children's sermon should place its moral imperatives in a context in which they are perceived as acts of love. If Jesus had come to make us good, then persuasion would be our objective. But since Jesus came to demonstrate God's great love, our goal is the acceptance of that love, which results in conversion.

The Trap of Humanism.   At the beginning of this discussion I spoke of the danger of being uncreative and literal in order to be biblical—that is, telling the old, old story as if it were a body of information to be mastered. Humanism is the other side of the coin: being overly original and "hip" can result in being humanistic. If moralism is the pitfall of conservatism, then humanism is the undertow of liberalism. A sermon may be moralistic and still be biblical (as long as the relationship between the indicative and the imperative is not consistently reversed), but it cannot be both humanistic and biblical. Fairy tales, fables, and anecdotes are generally humanistic. This does not make them unsuitable as a basis or starting point for a children's sermon; they simply cannot be the message. If moralism tends to confuse the Gospel with proper conduct or proper doctrine, humanism tends to confuse the Gospel with the wisdom of the ages or parental advice. The Bible is, of course, filled with the best kind of worldly wisdom, and the preacher has no difficulty in finding a suitable text to support humanistic truths. But the result is paramount to separating the message from the Messenger.

The Gospel without Jesus Christ is like a car without a motor: it looks attractive as long as it is standing still, but as soon as one tries to use it, its fatal flaw is discovered. Likewise, children may find humanistic sermons interesting and enjoy-

---

[11]Paul Scherer, *The Word God Sent* (New York: Harper & Row, 1965), pp. 15ff. This is still the best book I know of on the art of preaching.

able but completely useless outside of church, where wisdom quickly turns into expediency. If an individual has no ongoing relationship with Christ, imperatives to return evil with good and to avoid being anxious about tomorrow will only be lessons in frustration to him. No matter how it is dressed up, worldly wisdom will always be advice about how to get along in the world (*à la* Dale Carnegie), while God's foolishness is that which disrupts, reverses, and transforms (I Cor. 1-2).

THE STORY FORM AS PROCLAMATION

Using Storytelling in Gospel-Telling

Recently there has been considerable interest in the preacher as storyteller and the Gospel as God's story. Biblical studies have also strengthened the idea that the Bible not only is a book of stories but uses the story form as a distinctive way of proclaiming the Good News. Storytelling and Gospel-telling, then, are inextricably bound together. Frederick Buechner points out that the preacher need tell only two stories—his own and God's—and demonstrate where the two intersect.[12]

The story form seems a natural for children's sermons, not only because it is biblical but because children enjoy a good story. But we shouldn't embrace the art of storytelling without considerable clarification and qualification. We must remember that stories are a natural repository of metaphors, analogies, symbolic representation, and indirection—all of which pose particular problems for children. The story form is both alluring and allusive, stimulating and distracting, fascinating and fanciful. In short, it is a powerful tool of communication, but can be delusive in the wrong hands.

Amos Wilder has aptly stated the unique features of the story form in its purest sense:

> Now we know that a true metaphor or symbol is more than a sign, it is a bearer of the reality to which it

[12]Frederick Buechner's commencement address, "The Two Stories," published in Bangor Theological Seminary's *Open Door*, Summer 1980.

refers. The hearer not only learns about the reality, he participates in it. He is invaded by it. Here lies the power and fatefulness of art. Jesus' speech had the character not of instruction and ideas but of compelling imagination, of spell, of mythical shock and transformation. Not just in an aesthetic sense but in the service of the Gospel.[13]

Like Jesus' parables, a story draws in its listener and lets him participate in the action, almost without his knowing it. This is a story's alluring quality, and the benefits are considerable. "A large part of the power of the parable," writes John Shea, "is that you do not see it coming. Parable is blindside storytelling."[14] Unlike a moralistic story, which has a maxim that the listener anticipates long before it comes, the parabolic story teaches by indirection. The classic biblical example is Nathan's indirect indictment of David by way of a parable (II Sam. 12). In this instance Nathan's fear for his life ruled out directly confronting the king known for his angry outbursts. But the mode of communication he chose was effective because David permitted himself to come to terms with his conscience by "overhearing" the charge at a safe distance.

Telling Stories and "Overhearing the Gospel"

According to Fred Craddock, distance and participation are the two basic factors involved in "overhearing the Gospel."[15] Because the Gospel upsets all our conventional wisdom and challenges us to be more than we presently are, we are ambivalent about hearing what God wants to say to us. We would prefer to "listen in" at a safe distance so that we can beat a hasty retreat if necessary. In fact, we have always needed distance to deal with our unspoken fears. Children, for exam-

[13]Amos Wilder, *Early Christian Rhetoric: The Language of the Gospel* (Cambridge: Harvard University Press, 1971), p. 84. Richard A. Jensen's *Telling the Story* (Minneapolis: Augsburg, 1980) is a most helpful summary of this area of study and how it is applicable to the pulpit. Also very helpful is the book by John Shea, *Stories of God: An Unauthorized Biography* (Chicago: Thomas More Press, 1978)—particularly Chapter 5.

[14]Shea, *Stories of God*, p. 182.

[15]Fred B. Craddock, *Overhearing the Gospel* (Nashville: Abingdon, 1978), pp. 118.

ple, love certain types of ghost stories because they are real enough to voice children's inner thoughts but not so real that their spell cannot be broken by hiding under the covers or turning on a light. Experience has also taught us that adults are most attentive when listening to a children's story. In both instances the listener tunes in because he can participate at a safe distance—which is the psychology behind good storytelling. As a masterful storyteller, Jesus utilized this methodology of "overhearing the Gospel" to its fullest potential when he told parables. The power of the parable lies precisely in its ability to convince the hearer that he is listening to someone else's story. Consequently, he lowers his defenses and gets drawn into the story, discovering, at the climax, that *he is there*—that he is the one the story is about.

Every good storyteller realizes that he is most effective when he does not have to spell out the meaning of his story: the story itself carries its message best when the listener finds his own story within the one that is being told. The Bible is the unparalleled example of the way in which each generation retells the story of a previous generation in such a way that it discovers anew its own identity.[16]

Implicated in this process of overhearing and participation is an "empty space" which enables the listener to tell her own story. This characteristic of the parable/story is enhanced by its *open-ended* nature; unlike the object lesson, a good story is destroyed by over-explanation. Bruno Bettelheim, the noted psychiatrist, claims the relevance of the fairy tale lies in its open-ended character: "The fairy tale is therapeutic because the patient listener finds his own solutions through contemplating what the story seems to imply about him and his inner conflicts at this moment in his life."[17] Bettelheim then pro-

[16]I am especially appreciative of the way that Gerhard von Rad brings this to the fore in the Old Testament in *Old Testament Theology*, 2 vols. (New York: Harper & Row, 1962). It has become a valid thesis of biblical criticism, and especially of recent canonical criticism, to recover the hermeneutical process at work within the various traditions themselves. See, for example, James A. Sanders, *Torah and Canon* (Philadelphia: Fortress Press, 1972); and the introduction to James Sanders, *God Has a Story Too* (Philadelphia: Fortress Press, 1979).

[17]Bruno Bettelheim, *The Uses of Enchantment* (New York: Alfred A. Knopf, 1976), p. 25.

ceeds to show by carefully analyzing several classic fairy tales that, while some have a fixed conclusion (a happy ending), all have suggestive details that invite the listener to identify with the characters, and all leave many questions unanswered. Why, for example, does the "innocent" Red Riding Hood disobey her mother and stray from the path and get cornered by the nasty old wolf? The story raises this question but does not answer it. Thus the fairy tale is distinctive because, unlike fables and moralistic stories, it teaches by encouraging the listener/participant to explore what might happen if she disobeys the rules or acts upon her fantasies or fears.

Becoming a Good Storyteller

Can there be any doubt that a well-formulated story is ideally suited to convey the Good News to children? It works not so much because it conveys new content or holds up an exemplary model, but because it is experiential and allows for self-recognition. John Dominic Crossan explains the difficulty of the challenge facing us when we try to become good storytellers:

> It is one thing to communicate to others conclusions and admonition based upon one's own profound spiritual experience. It was this that Pharisaic theology did so admirably at the time of Jesus. It is quite another thing to try and communicate that experience itself, or, better, to assist people to find their own ultimate encounter. This is what Jesus' parables seek to do: to help others into their own experience of the Kingdom and to draw from that experience their own way of life.[18]

This quotation recalls the distinction between the indicative and the imperative. Because of the unique qualities of the story form—because it is indirect and open-ended, because it allows distance and involvement—it naturally proves itself to be an effective form of communication. But these qualities can be subverted to teach good behavior or to turn Jesus into a moralistic instructor. The story form will be no better than

[18]John Dominic Crossan, *In Parables* (New York: Harper & Row, 1973), p. 52.

other forms of communication if we use it to admonish children instead of employing it to help them experience God's love.

One of my earlier attempts to be creative in the art of storytelling was the sermon entitled "A Prince in Disguise." I have since concluded that it may not have been very meaningful for younger children but was much better than an object lesson about treating others as we would treat Christ. "Baa-Baa," a story told with figures on a flannel board and aimed at younger children, is a very different example. The crucial issue in both stories is whether the children identified with the characters and were thus drawn into the drama. If this happened, then I as the storyteller gave them an extended metaphor which could evoke (and evoke repeatedly) the experience inherent in the story.

Because stories tend to become long and involved, I urge telling stories which are straightforward, and simple in plot and in structure. Autobiographical stories should not be ruled out. In two published books of children's sermons Jerry Jordan relates the Gospel by using almost exclusively autobiographical stories and anecdotes (sometimes using objects to introduce the stories). I have no quarrel with his basic reasoning: this style is intimate and direct, and inspires the listeners to draw upon their own personal experiences. But unlike the anecdote, the parable/story has the power to create its own experience, and this is important if our stories are going to lift children out of their usual experience of love and into a new experience of love as Christ defined it. The question we must continually be asking ourselves is whether the story stands alone and does what it can do best.

Avoiding Storytelling Pitfalls

We must try to avoid three general pitfalls as we attempt to become good storytellers. The first is our old friend moralism. Either because we misunderstand Jesus' use of parables or because we have been influenced by Aesop's fables or fairy tales from childhood, we favor stories with a moral. Consequently, we fail to illumine the Christian motivation behind

some ethical behavior and run the risk of isolating the imperative from the indicative.

Secondly, stories frequently require the listener to move
from the past to the present or from the present to the past,
from the particular to the universal or from the universal to the
particular. When a narrative involves a fictional character in a
faraway place, the child is required to make such an effort—
one that she will not always make—in order to translate the
message into her particular situation. And whenever we try to
adapt a story which is not our own, we always run the risk of
losing the realism that was conveyed by the setting which belongs to the original story. Jesus was an effective communica-
tor because his stories were set in a world in which matter-of-
fact things happened (sheep got lost, lepers were segregated),
people did ordinary things (kept the law, attended marriage
feasts), and one action led to another (those who worked on the
Sabbath were rebuked, sons demanded their inheritance and
left home). A successful story depends upon a setting which
does not call attention to itself but which enhances the drama
by causing the listener to think, "Yes, that could happen to
me."

Thirdly, most contemporary stories suffer from being too
complete; stories work best when they allow the listener to
recognize himself. We seem to forget how many of Jesus'
parable-stories are open-ended (we are never told the fate of
the prodigal son's older brother, or of the woman caught in the
act of adultery), or how many begin or end with a question
(Luke 12:42; 17:7ff; Matt. 12:11).[19]

At its best the parable-story shows the listener his great potential for both love and destruction (*simul justus et peccator*),
doing so by asking the question and posing the challenge.
When the listener is "put on the spot" in this way, he is most
likely to learn something about himself. How totally different
from the usual object lesson is a story which invites the

[19]We must take into account the tendency of the early church to close off
the open-ended quality of Jesus' style of teaching by appending their own interpretation or by transposing the story into a new context. See Crossan, *In
Parables*, and Joachim Jeremias, *The Parables of Jesus* (New York: Charles
Scribner's Sons, 1963; rev. ed. 1971).

listener's participation and identification and then compels him to make a decision that charts his future course! How different from the usual moralism that is supposed to lay before him the correct path to follow and therefore relieves him from the seriousness of his own decision concerning which master to follow!

GETTING STARTED: CONTROLLING
THE CREATIVE PROCESS

Where to start? How to begin? These can be two troublesome questions. One approach would have the minister/teacher start with a creative idea or an object and work backward to a message. It will sometimes work to begin this way, but most of the time it won't. I have learned that it is best to begin with the Scriptural message for Sunday's worship. This provides the primary impetus for a biblically based sermon, but it also disciplines and focuses my creative thinking and prayer life. In addition, it makes the worship service a cohesive experience. And I often discover that the children's sermon gives me the freedom to say something to the entire congregation which might seem inappropriate in a strictly adult context.

Next I write down the sermon's purpose, and then check it against the Scriptural passage to make sure that I don't stray from the text. I also apply my exegesis and study for the adult sermon to the children's sermon. But I don't consider this step finished until I have asked, How does the biblical message relate to these children? What is their experience of its truth? I find my own children very helpful at this stage, because I can try out my ideas on them; without them I would have to find another way to probe the world of children. During this step I am also deciding which age group I will primarily address. Finally, I may have to refine or rework the purpose of the sermon according to the particular audience I am addressing.

It is at this point that I try to be creative, although it is not wise to try to force creativity. Creativity is more likely to spring from a source in a way that is impossible to define. Nevertheless, I have charged and channeled the creative impulse in my groundwork. I also give my ideas at least several days to "brew," my goal being to develop a medium which is particularly well-suited to the message and thoroughly engaging. A pantomime, for example, will be appropriate only for a certain message and text. So if I choose the form first, without considering its relationship to my message, I may still be wondering what to say on Sunday morning, or look foolish because the form (the creative impulse) and the content don't connect.

Because many individuals use the various media—such as movies and television—more skillfully and creatively than I do, I am always on the lookout for their good ideas. I can store them up just as I can develop a repertoire of ideas for adult sermons by reading. But I always remember the golden rule: never let the idea predominate over the biblical message.

CONCLUSIONS

1. Do not teach children anything that they will need to relearn later.

2. Always include the day-to-day experience of the children you are addressing.

3. Beware of biblical accounts originally meant for adults. Be conscious of the *literal interpretation* that children will give a biblical story.

4. Make sure that each sermon has one and only one point; remember that you need only one "portable" idea to be effective.

5. Place each children's sermon within a context: (a) within the service of worship, which develops a central theme; (b) within the curriculum of the Sunday school; (c) within a curriculum related to the lectionary; or (d) within a long-range plan for leading the congregation.

6. Remember that sermons with the greatest impact are those which actively and physically involve the listener; next greatest in impact are those which can be seen as well as heard. Remember the learning pyramid.

7. Know the basic differences between pre-school, elementary-school, and older elementary-school children. Then decide how best to target your sermon so that it will challenge some and be understood by most.

8. Watch your language. Be aware that although analogies and allegories may be clear to you, they will probably confuse children.

9. Ask yourself two questions: Am I trivializing the Gospel by focusing on character-building (moralism), or neglecting the One who empowers us to overcome hate with love (humanism)?

10. Tell the Story in such a way that children experience God's love as radical reversal and surprising joy.

PART II

Children's Sermons and Gospel-Telling

The following definitions and classifications affect the shape and the groupings of the sermons included in this section.

DEFINITIONS

Object Lesson

An object lesson is one in which the object is central and indispensable to the lesson being taught. Not all children's sermons which employ an object are necessarily object lessons. The distinction depends upon whether the object is necessary or merely serves as a tangible reference for an abstract idea, a starting point, or an illustration of some aspect of the homily. For example, it is possible to tell the story of Jesus' birth without any object, with a single object, or with an array of objects. But the telling of the story becomes an object lesson, only when a single specific object, such as swaddling clothes, is the primary means by which the minister draws the listener into faith about the Incarnation. In many ways the distinction between sign and symbol comes into play here, because in one instance the object is merely a sign, but in other instances the object is or becomes an avenue of participation (a symbol).

Sign vs. Symbol

The distinction between sign and symbol is predicated upon the degree of the involvement of the listener/observer. A sign, such as a directional signal or an algebraic notation, merely points to (refers to) another object or condition which is not immediately evident. A symbol, on the other hand, not only indicates something but represents it in some intrinsic way. A symbol is unique in that normal boundaries between different realities are blurred (as they are, for example, in a dream), because to understand a symbol implies being involved or be-coming involved in it (Paul Ricoeur).

A cross, for instance, would be only a sign to a nonbeliever, pointing or referring to a historical event (the death of a man named Jesus). But the Cross would be a symbol to believers, who might be willing to die for what it represents —namely, the incarnation of God's love in Jesus, the Messiah. As preachers and teachers of the Word, our aim is not so much to turn objects into signs but to transform signs (and images) into symbols which repeatedly involve us in that which they symbolize.

Simile, Allegory, Metaphor

A simile is a concise figure of speech that directly compares two usually unrelated things to indicate a likeness between them— e.g., "All we like sheep have gone astray" (Isa. 53:6). An allegory necessarily involves the listener in a decoding process. A story is told, a pictorial representation is given, which sug-gests a central truth, thus augmenting and deepening the meaning of the lesson. The parable of the sower (Mark 4:3-8), for example, preserves a story which had become allegorized in the classical sense; its point-for-point interpretation follows (vs. 14-20; cf. Ezek. 17:3-10, 11-21).

Like a simile, a metaphor vitalizes speech by juxtaposing two usually unrelated things in order to make one or both more vivid. Unlike an allegory or a simile, a metaphor accomplishes its goal by making the comparison implicitly. When St. Paul speaks of Christ crucified as a stumbling block unto the Jews (I Cor. 1:23), he is forming a metaphor because the meaning that is implied depends upon bringing together the idea of the Messiah *and* death by crucifixion—each acceptable in its own right but in combination certainly unthinkable to a Jewish population awaiting a King who would sit on David's throne. Of course, this metaphor could be extended in many ways—in a story or a parable, for example.

A simile most often uses the conjunctive "like," while a metaphor employs the predicate "is." Thus we have several levels of abstraction as we move from simple description to simile to metaphor:

> God is strong and gentle.
> God is strong and gentle *like* a shepherd.
> The Lord *is* my shepherd.

Story

There are many kinds of story forms: legends, sagas, parables, paradigms, analogies, fantasies, fairy tales, fables, myths, plays, novels, anecdotes, and miracles. Despite the variety of forms, a story always has characters, a plot, and a setting; the better these are defined, the better the story. Likewise, a story can serve various purposes, without one excluding another: it can simultaneously teach, moralize, dramatize, illustrate, argue, excite, and provoke. It is important, then, for the storyteller to be conscious of what form he chooses and what purpose he has in mind when he communicates in this way.

Parable

Definitions of a parable range from "a short riddle" to "a fully developed allegory." I use a definition that is gaining acceptance among biblical scholars because it considerably restricts the style and function of a parable as it was used by Jesus.[1] A parable is a particular kind of story which, by using metaphor, allegory, or some other device, communicates by making the listener a participant in the action. Both the parable and the metaphor serve a similar purpose: they suggest a deeper reality, unveil a hidden mystery, or reveal an unrealized potential. For this reason a parable can be thought of as an extended metaphor. Nathan's confronting King David with a parable (II Sam. 12:1-7) demonstrates the power of this form of communication to lead the listener to make a new discovery and recognize a new possibility for his life.

John Shea observes that some parables function as similes and others as metaphors; there are no hard-and-fast rules for defining their function because the hearer's response often determines it.[2] There is, so to speak, a continuum of listener

[1] John Dominic Crossan, *In Parables* (New York: Harper & Row, 1973). In my estimation, this is the most helpful book contributing to understanding the parables of Jesus.

[2] John Shea, *Stories of God: An Unauthorized Biography* (Chicago: Thomas More Press, 1978).

participation. More than a simple transliteration is required at the level of parable-metaphor: a cognitive/emotive jump into a new dimension is necessary. When parables function merely as simile, they *illustrate* the redemptive process. But when they function as metaphor, the parables of Jesus are powerful stories which *reverse* our natural attitudes and actions.

The distinction is now being made between parables or stories of *participation* and stories of *illustration.* The latter is the category in which most sermon illustrations belong. The preacher/teacher uses a story or a metaphor to illustrate a point, and once the point is made, the illustration has served its function. A parable, as we are defining it, differs because it attempts to make the listener aware of a referent so new or so alien that she is required to participate to some degree. Thus the purpose of a parable is not to give information but to help the listener transcend her present situation so that she can process information in a new way.

As we communicate the Gospel of Jesus Christ, we will give less than our best if we lose this distinction between forms of communication which restrict experience in order to make it palatable, and those which are an experience in themselves —an experience which offers the listener a new conception of the world.

CLASSIFICATIONS

Because I intend this volume to be a handbook of ideas and methods, I have arranged the sermons according to type instead of by theme or season. Below are my classifications, which are by no means absolute.

Let's Pretend: A sermon which requires the listeners to use their imaginations in a vivid way.

Visual Demonstration: A sermon in which an object is intrinsic to the message. The object may begin as a sign but may later become a symbol that evokes the original occasion of the sermon.

Dramatic Participation: A sermon given in the tradition of the parable which requires the listeners' actual participation in the drama.

The Pantomime and the Echo: Sermons which require the listeners to process non-verbal clues and use their imaginations.

The Story: A sermon with a well-defined plot and characters. (This form is one of the most difficult to use successfully; the above forms should probably be mastered first.)

The Prophets: Sermons intended to exemplify the meaning of the term "prophetic" in both biblical and contemporary settings.

LET'S PRETEND

These sermons require the listeners to use their imaginations in a vivid way.

Stilling the Storm

Text: Matthew 8:23-27
Season: Any
Summary: Like the disciples, we must learn to trust the Lord.

Preparation: Begin by showing the children a picture of Jesus stilling the storm or another picture depicting a storm in its full fury.

This morning I'm asking you to join me in a "let's-pretend" game. These games are a great way for us to recreate a special mood or situation. With your help this morning we can tell the story of how the disciples learned to trust Jesus, especially when they felt frightened and forsaken. The story is commonly known as Jesus stilling the storm, and to recreate the story I'll need a few of you to add some important sound effects. (Choose a sufficient number of children to create the sound of wind, and others to create the sound of water; their cue is your mention of these elements. Have the two groups rehearse once or twice, mentioning that you will act as their volume control by raising or lowering your hand. Have the remaining children form themselves into a boat, leaving an empty space for Jesus. Be sure the sound-effects group is as close as possible to the "boat" so that they are part of the total drama.)

At the end of the day, when the sun was setting, Jesus and his disciples began to cross the Sea of Galilee. Suddenly, out of nowhere, great black clouds covered the sky, and it grew very dark. The wind began to blow, and the sea began to rise and rock the boat. The disciples thought the storm would pass over soon, because they didn't see how it could become worse. But the storm grew even fiercer—the wind blew harder, and the waves poured over the side of the boat. The boat began to fill with water, and the disciples thought for sure their boat would sink and they would all be drowned.

They were frightened, and they felt alone! But Jesus was asleep in the back of the boat, his head resting on a cushion. Imagine that: while the wind blew fiercely and the waves slapped against the boat, Jesus was not even a little bit afraid because he had so much trust in God.

The disciples rushed to wake Jesus up. And when Jesus realized how frightened the disciples were, he commanded the wind and the water to be still—and they were quiet. Then Jesus turned to his disciples and asked them, "Why are you afraid? If you believe in God, know that God is all-powerful and can surely be trusted to care for us no matter what happens to us."

Note: The content of let's-pretend stories is less important than the feelings they generate. Keeping in mind that children are particularly good at using their imaginations, you can think of a number of Gospel stories that lend themselves to this mode of Gospel-telling: the stories of the boy Jesus in the temple (Luke 2), the ten lepers (Luke 17), the feeding of the five thousand (Matt. 14), the widow's mite (Luke 21), Jesus' visit to Mary and Martha (Luke 10), Jesus washing the feet of his disciples (John 13), and Jesus' cleansing of the temple (Matt. 21); and the parables of the great banquet (Luke 14), the sower (Mark 4), and of the lost coin, the lost lamb, and the lost son (Luke 15). Most of these stories also involve parabolic action through which the Gospel is enacted. Be sure to define your characters carefully, as you do for role-playing stories; then children will feel more comfortable about participating. You should define the roles first, and then let children "feel" their parts. They can add their own definitions of their characters later on.

Death Comes to the Henry Family

Text: John 14:1ff.
Season: Any
Summary: Through death, we enter God's eternal Kingdom.
(Children have the capacity to understand this basic Christian message.)
Props: Flannel-graph and figures: mother and father (I prefer mother and father grouped as one, representing the parental figure; this also makes the role easier to play and more adaptable for single-parent families); Judy (in junior high), Michael (6 years old), and Sharon (4 years old). Figures can be cut from a magazine and backed with felt or masking tape.

Preparation: Begin by introducing each person and giving his age.

Scene I *(Mother, Father, and Judy)*
Mother: We sure will miss grandma around here.
Father: Yes, we will. We knew she was sick and might die soon, but just the same, I wish she could have lived a few more years. What's bothering me is *what* we should tell Michael and Sharon.
Mother: I think we should wait to tell them. You know how the children loved their grandmother.
Judy: I think we should tell them now—they have a right to know.
Mother: You're right, of course, but I don't know if they'll understand what has happened.

54

Father: Does it really matter if they understand everything? They'll understand enough in their own way.

Scene II *(add Michael and Sharon)*
Michael and Sharon: We heard. We heard you and mommy talking. Did grandma really die?
Father: Yes, she did. She died last night.
Michael: Does that mean we'll never see her again? Has she gone away to see God?
Sharon: I want to see grandma. I want to see her now.
Mother: We can't see her, Sharon. It's going to be hard but we'll have to learn to live our lives without grandma from now on.
Sharon: I don't care. I want to be with her.
Father: I know it isn't easy for you to understand, but grandma has gone to a different world—a world you've never seen before, but a world where you can be very, very close to God.
Judy: I never thought of it like that before, but death is like a bridge.* The only way we can cross over to God's world is by passing over the bridge of death.
Michael: I wish I could see what God's Kingdom is like.
Mother: Someday I know you will, but for the moment you'll have to enjoy God's Kingdom as it is here on earth.
Judy: Does God have two Kingdoms?
Mother: No, Judy. I didn't mean to confuse everyone. When Jesus came to earth he started a Kingdom based upon love— one that includes our world and grandma's world. You might even say that we are trying to help God complete that Kingdom every time we love instead of hate.
Judy: But grandma doesn't have to wait any longer, does she? She's already there.
Father: I guess you could put it that way. Grandma is now able to love God with all her heart and mind and spirit.
Michael: I know grandma won't be able to take us on any

---

*Throughout the conversation I have avoided using language that implies that death is like sleep or that God's eternal Kingdom is a place with a specific location. Both analogies are unbiblical and teach children concepts which they must relearn later. Listen to other people's discussions of death, and you will discover how common these two notions are.

more trips, but I'm glad she crossed over that bridge to be closer to God.

Father: The Bible doesn't answer all of our questions about death, but it does promise the most important thing. Death is the end of one journey, but it is also the beginning of a new one. God showed us that when Jesus was raised from the dead. We'll be sad that grandma is gone, but thankful that God will give grandma a new life in a world where love is everywhere.

Note: The power of this type of sermon comes from the situation itself: the children are allowed to listen in as another family talks about a very sensitive subject (see Part I, "The Story Form as Proclamation").

Show Me How Strong You Are

Text: Matthew 5:38-42; Luke 23:34
Season: Lent, any season
Summary: The stronger you are, the more you can love someone who is hating you.
Setting: This sermon works best in a setting where children feel free to be themselves.

Preparation: Divide the group into two equal parts. Ask for several volunteers from each group (include both boys and girls). Next ask one group of volunteers to think of themselves as playground bullies. Have them assume a pose of toughness and meanness toward the other group of volunteers. Being sure the two groups are directly facing each other, ask the "victims" what they would like to do in return. Have them assume poses representing their feelings. Then ask the "bullies" what they would do next; include, as well, children from the rest of their group who are still seated. Ask them all how long this would continue— until one group had proven that they were stronger than the other? Next have the volunteers sit down with their own groups, reminding them that they have a pretended membership in one group or the other.

Now let's pretend what would happen if one group had a powerful laser gun, and the other group had one, too. And for some reason, whether by accident or on purpose, this group fired on you. What would you do? (Be prepared for some non-traditional answers.)

Going even further, let's pretend that instead of laser guns we had atomic bombs. This group over here has just fired its laser gun and killed many of your people. And if they drop their bomb on you, are you going to stand by and take that? What are you going to do? (Be free to flow with the children's logic. They may very well come up with a peaceful solution.)

If you remember, we began with a seemingly innocent playground fight, and now we have a world war on our hands. Jesus said he understood that we have learned to act that way: an eye for an eye, and a tooth for a tooth. So I ask you, How do we change the way we and everyone else acts? (Pause, then begin a discussion, guiding it toward the question of who is the stronger person: the one who begins a fight or the one who avoids returning insult for insult, blow for blow.)

We might not usually think of Jesus as the strongest person in the world, because we usually associate strength with fists and armies and bombs. Aren't we supposed to be the strongest nation in the world because we have the best weapons of destruction? Because Jesus knew very well how it is with the world, he decided to give us an example of how to change the way we act when someone is out to hurt us or hate us. He knew he had to do more than just tell us to return love for hate. So Jesus, when they had nailed him to a cross to die, looked out among those who had wanted him crucified, and said, "Father, forgive them; for they know not what they are doing."

You will have to decide for yourself whether Jesus was the strongest person in the world and what it means to be the strongest nation in the world. I can truthfully say that the world is waiting for your answer!

Note: This sermon ends by inviting a response which the children must complete "in their own time and in their own way." This type of sermon should not be turned into a moralistic teaching but left open-ended. The inviting itself is a characteristic of good storytelling and Jesus' parables.

VISUAL DEMONSTRATIONS

In these sermons an object is intrinsic to the message. The object may begin as a sign but may later become a symbol that evokes the original occasion of the sermon.

Three Persons, Three Sides

Text: Matthew 28:19, II Corinthians 13:14
Appropriate Day: Trinity Sunday
Summary: We can understand the Trinity as a triangle.
Props: An equilateral triangle made out of cardboard

Sometimes we parents are not as smart as we would like to be. We find it very difficult to understand how God can be Father, Son, and Holy Spirit. How can one person—even if he *is* God—be three persons? Or how can three persons be the same person? It's a very perplexing problem. Sometimes we even get so confused that we aren't sure whether we're praying to Jesus or to God.

To help us understand the Trinity—which is a word we use to speak about God the Creator, God the Savior, and God the Holy Spirit*—I've made a triangle. This triangle has three different but equal sides, and yet all three sides are needed in order to make it a triangle. Perhaps it would help if we now named each side. On this side I'll write the word "Creator" or "Father," and on this side "Savior" or "Son," and on the third side I'll write "Holy Spirit." As I turn the triangle, we can see one name but not the others, yet we know that the other two names or sides are still there. (Illustrate this idea by turning the triangle around slowly.) And this is how we experience God:

*I began with the traditional phraseology "Father, Son, and Holy Spirit," but then changed to a phraseology which may very well be more biblical and also steers clear of the masculine emphasis of the traditional formula.

either as Creator, or as our Savior, Jesus Christ, or as the Holy Spirit—but not all three persons at once. And when we do experience God in one particular way, it doesn't mean we can't experience him differently at some other time.

Perhaps it would also help if we named this last side, which is the bottom if we place the triangle on the table like this (illustrate "sitting" triangle). On the bottom I'll write the word "God" because "God" is the word we use to talk about all three aspects of God at once. Just as we use the word "triangle" to refer to the whole triangle, so we use the word "God" to refer to all three sides of God.

We began by saying that sometimes we get confused about whether we should pray to God or to Jesus Christ. But if we think of this triangle, we see that when we pray to Jesus Christ we *are* praying to God. Jesus Christ is only one side of God, one way to understand him, just as the Holy Spirit (turning the triangle) is another way to understand God, and God the Creator (turning the triangle) is yet a different way. This is what we mean, then, when we say that God is three persons in one. God is God the Creator, God the Savior, and God the Holy Spirit.

The Cross and "I"

Text: Mark 8:34; 10:43-45; I Corinthians 13:5
Appropriate Day: Passion Sunday, any Sunday
Props: An American flag and a small cross made of two notched pieces of wood which you can hang around your neck (something you can make quite easily with soft wood and a coping saw).

I've brought with me today two well-known symbols. The first is an American flag; the other is a cross.

Let me begin by asking what comes to your mind when you see the American flag. . . . In some ways the American flag means different things to each of us, depending upon our experience of what it is to be an American. And yet, for all of us the flag is a symbol that brings together all of those feelings. When we see the American flag, we can say, "That is what it means to be an American."*

Now I'll ask what you think of when you see this symbol (holding up the cross you have made). . . . Again, we find that the symbol of the cross brings out in us a variety of feelings and responses, but we almost always connect the cross with words like "love," "sacrifice," "suffering," and "death." The cross, then, has a special meaning to those of us who are Christians, because it reminds us that Jesus loved everyone so much that he "crossed himself out" when he did for us on the cross.

*You can also effectively introduce this theme by having the children find the best-known symbol of Christianity in the sanctuary, then asking why this is so.

THE CROSS AND "I"

The cross I have hanging around my neck is one that I made. ⁺ As I take it off you can see that it comes apart. The longer piece looks like the capital letter "I," while the other piece crosses the "I" out (demonstrate). This is exactly what Jesus did when he allowed himself to be nailed to a wooden cross: he crossed himself out. In other words, he showed us that love means putting yourself last, or crossing yourself out for the sake of another person.

I know that you can think of many times—when you're fighting with your brother or sister or playing with a friend—when you insist upon having your own way. "I'm the one that counts," you think. "It's what I want to do." "Do it my way, stupid!" you might shout. "I want my way, right now!"

Saint Paul writes that love does not insist upon its own way. And you are showing love those many times when you *do* put yourself last. It is not easy to cross the "me" out, but when we love someone, that is exactly what we do.

You will never find a Christian church without a cross, because it is one symbol above all other symbols that reminds us how Jesus loved us. He crossed himself out—and as this cross shows you (demonstrate again) the meaning of God's love is built right into the symbol.

Go in peace, knowing that in Jesus Christ God loved us with all that he had.

⁺ In a less formal setting you can have each child make his own two-part cross as a necklace. To keep the cross from becoming just another piece of jewelry, I would have the children promise to show others its hidden meaning.

The Great Commandment

Text: Matthew 22:37-40 (The Great Commandment)
Season: Any
Summary: The essence of Christianity is the love between God and man and between people.
Props: The same cross you made for "The Cross and 'I'"

It is sometimes very easy to get confused about what it means to be a Christian. Every time you come to church I hope you learn something new, and I suspect that sometimes you aren't sure what is the most important teaching for your life. Jesus knew this might happen, so he gave us one great commandment. If we can remember this one great commandment it will always be easy to know what God expects of us, because we will always know that it is the most important thing about our Christian faith.

The great commandment that Jesus gave us is this: "You shall love the Lord your God with all your heart, and with all your soul, and with all your mind. And, you shall love your neighbor as yourself."

This great commandment is not really very hard to learn, but it would be helpful if we had a sign or a symbol to get us started. It so happens that we do have a symbol—the cross itself. I'm wearing the wooden cross that I made so that you can see how a cross is two pieces that come apart (pulling the two pieces apart). Most of you will remember that this part is the "I," and this part crosses the "I" out (demonstrate). This is what Jesus did when he died upon the cross, and it is what we must do if we're going to love God and our neighbor. We can also think of the cross as two pointers. The longer part points to the love between God and man, and the shorter part points to the love between people.

What, then, is the very heart of Christianity? It is to love God with all that we are—and this pointer reminds us of the first part of the great commandment—and to love others just as we love ourselves—and this pointer should help us remember the second part of the great commandment (demonstrate). And when we put the two pointers together, we have a cross. So we have both a great commandment and a symbol to keep us from getting confused. And what is amazing is that both are the same (holding up the cross).

This morning I'm going to lay my wooden cross on the communion table under the larger silver cross. It's my way of saying to God, "I understand that you want me to cross myself out so I can better love You and everyone I meet."

Note: In reviewing this sermon I realized that we as humans become this cross when we stretch out our arms. Just as children make angels in the snow by lying on their backs and swinging their arms, so they could see the symbolism of standing with their heads pointing toward God and their arms reaching out to their neighbors. With this simple action they could directly participate in the sermon.

A Book of Words/The Book of Love

Text: John 20:30-31
Season: Any
Summary: The Bible is the book most important to us when
we want to learn about love.
Props: A dictionary

The English language is made up of a lot of words. In school
you're finding out just how many words there are. And when
you get stuck, wondering how to spell a word or how to define
a particular word, you find a dictionary. I happen to have one
here—it's Webster's Third International Dictionary. It's quite
a large book, as you can see. In fact, it has 450,000 entries and
2,662 pages. As you can see, no one can know all the words in
the English language, so it's very helpful to have a dictionary.

What do you think is the most *important* word in the
English language? (Have several children respond; a few will
probably say "love.") Those are all good answers, and some of
you agree with me. I, too, think the word "love" is the most
important word we have. Would anyone know how many
times we find the word "love" in this dictionary? One
time—that's right, one time—on page 1,340. So this dictionary
isn't much help when it comes to finding the *most important*
word, because it simply lists every word only once.

But if we turn to this book (taking down the pulpit Bible),
which is just as big, we find that the word "love" is used almost
600 times! Let me read just a few of the important passages
that speak about love:

You shall love the Lord your God with all your heart, and with all your soul, and with all your might (Deut. 6:5).

You shall love your neighbor as yourself (Lev. 19:18).

God's steadfast love endures forever (Ps. 136:1).

Greater love has no man than this, that a man lay down his life for his friends (John 15:13).

Even if I speak in the tongue of men and of angels, but have not love, I am a noisy gong or a clanging cymbal (I Cor. 13:1).

There can be little doubt that "love" is the most important word in this book. And that's why it is often called the Book of Love.

I think we've learned something this morning that we already knew. The most important word in our lives is love—love that is given to us by God, our parents, our friends, and even by strangers. Life would be completely different if we could not give love and receive love. And we also learned that the Bible is *the* book to turn to when we want to learn more about love.

May the love of God the Creator, God the Redeemer, and God the Holy Spirit be with you all.

Giving Love a Chance

Text: Matthew 5:43ff; (Romans 12:9ff); I Corinthians 12:3ff.
Season: Any
Summary: We need to give love more of a chance to work.
Setting: Place a toy gun and a Bible on a table. If possible, have the table in a place where the children must pass by it. Keep in mind that a very formal setting may work against you. A chapel service, for example, might be more appropriate than a church service.

Preparation: Begin by making some reference to what happened as the children walked by the table displaying the gun and the Bible. Ask them which of the two is more powerful.

The gun, as you know, has the power to kill someone. The Bible doesn't have that power, so people aren't afraid of it. But I wonder. If you wanted to conquer the world, which of these would you choose? With this gun you could make people afraid. With this Bible you could teach them about God's love and the way Jesus loved other people. You could win the world over by changing people's hearts rather than by bossing them around.

I hope that no one here will ever feel he must own a gun in order to control another person. But even though you don't own a gun, there are times when you pinch, bite, hit, or put someone down because you don't know any other way to change that person. Using force looks like the quick, easy way to do it, and that's why we so often choose it over love and forgiveness.

There is a better way, writes Saint Paul in First Corinthians. We all know the better way is to love the person with whom we are angry—whom we might even hate for the moment. We lose control, we lose our cool, and we try to use force. We know from experience that kindness doesn't usually get very quick results.

I believe everyone in this chapel knows that love is more powerful than guns or force. We just don't have the patience for love. It is harder, and it does take longer to convince someone you love him or her. Your sister or brother ought to know that you love them, but they begin to have doubts the second your caring gives way to yelling and hitting. Sisters and brothers, mothers and dads—even governments and nations—know that patience and love is a better way, but their trust is also easily shaken. So you see, we all need to be a little more patient and a lot more trusting in the power of love.

Let us pray: "Dear loving God, you trusted in love when you sent your only Son into this world. Help us to trust you more and more, to make your love our taproot and foundation. Amen."

Note: A gun, even a toy gun, is a strong—even disturbing—visual image. You will have to use your own discretion about it, based upon your particular situation and the setting. On the other hand, the gun and the Bible become visual signs of the choice between love and violence. And because the sermon offers an either/or choice, the Bible or the gun, you are forcing a decision, a characteristic of Jesus' use of parables. Learning usually happens as the result of conflict resolution, so I would not back away from setting up a moral dilemma. But the real accent of this sermon is not the moral choice but the patience and perseverance needed when love does not pay back immediate dividends.

My original conclusion had you moving to the table and picking up first the gun and then the Bible and saying, "With this you are tempted to think you can conquer the world. With this you know that it is love that conquers all, even bratty brothers and sisters." The accent would then shift to the moral choice.

The Gift of Giving

Text: John 3:16
Appropriate Day or Season: Advent, Christmas Eve
Summary: Advent/Christmas is a time for us to decide
again whether we will accept God's gift of Jesus.
Props: Prepare a fairly large box, wrapped for Christmas,
which contains a crèche (as many figures as you wish).

What do you like best about Christmas? That's a hard question
to answer, because so many things about it make us excited. I
do know for sure that you're excited about the presents you're
going to receive. Christmas morning is really a special time,
with your stockings filled from the toe to the top, and piles of
presents under the tree.

But let's think for a moment about the fun we have *giving*
presents. I'm not one-hundred percent sure about this, but I
think I enjoy giving gifts more than I enjoy receiving them.
When I've taken the time to choose or make a special gift for
someone I love, I tingle all over in anticipation. Will they like
the present? Will they know how much of myself is in that gift?

Perhaps you've made a special gift; or perhaps you've
bought a special gift with money you've saved. And on
Christmas morning you will try to wait patiently to give it, and
your heart will pound loudly when your gift is about to be
opened. If we can talk about God in human terms—and I
think we can—then I think we can say that God had feelings
like these when he gave the world the gift of his Son.

Since I like to give presents so much, I've brought one in today.* I would guess that you've already spotted it, and are wondering if it's for you. Well, it's for all of you (the tag reads: "To all the children of the Church"). I know some of you would like to help me open it. (As the present is being unwrapped, add a note of caution: "I can already see that this box has one gift inside—one gift for everyone"; otherwise, children may expect something they can take home for their very own.) I can also see that this gift has several parts to it, each one carefully wrapped. This figure must be Joseph, and this one Mary. Here is a small crib, and here is the baby Jesus.

The gift in this box, then, is God's special gift given to all of us—the baby Jesus who grew up to be the Christ who sacrificed himself on a cross. I'm sure a few of you are thinking how much you would like to take this present home and give it a place of honor. But since we want everyone in the church to see this beautiful scene of Jesus' birth, we'll set it up here on top of the piano. Nevertheless, I do hope that you'll take this present home, and that you'll carry it *in your hearts* everywhere you go, because God wanted you to have the gift of his Son in your hearts all the time.

This season of Advent is a very good time for us to remember just how much God likes giving gifts. I hope that this Christmas you will enjoy giving a gift to someone you love. And I hope you'll remember that, no matter how much you enjoy both giving and receiving gifts, God has enjoyed many times more giving the gift of his Son to you and to the world. With eager anticipation God waits to see if we are willing to accept his gift. It was, after all, a very costly gift: a son who suffered many things so that we might be more giving and loving ourselves.

*Since Advent is about anticipation, you might prefer to "display" the gift in the chancel for the Advent period, and then open it on Christmas Eve (if you have a service that night), or on the last Sunday in Advent.

You Can't Steal a Spirit

Text: Matthew 2:1-12; 6:19-21
Appropriate Day: Epiphany or the Sunday after Christmas
Summary: The spirit of Christmas will last because every Sunday we celebrate God's gift of Jesus.
Props: A box of old toys (wrap the box in holiday paper)

Christmas is over, and that means the end of some things. No more surprises. No more guessing what presents we're getting. Although it's true that Christmas Day won't come for another 3___ days, the Church celebrates the coming of the Wise Men from the East on January 6th. This Sunday is known as Epiphany, and in the Greek Orthodox Church gifts are not unwrapped until this day in remembrance of the gifts that the Wise Men brought to the baby Jesus. I know we would like Christmas to last . . . and last . . . and last. But it can't—or can it?

On the church steps I see a Christmas present that's still wrapped, so maybe there is hope that Christmas can last. Let's open it and see what's in it. Let me see . . . this box seems to be filled with several gifts, and they're not exactly new. My guess is that they're last year's Christmas presents. Actually, a few of them look like they're several years old. This game has lost its marbles, so it isn't much fun any more. This book has seen better days, and it won't last much longer. And this doll has lost one of its arms.

You may say that wasn't much of a present—and you're

right. I must confess that I was the one who brought the box in last night. I was thinking about one of my favorite Christmas T.V. specials: "How the Grinch Stole Christmas." Even though I've seen it many times, every Christmas I find myself watching it just one more time. As you probably remember, the Grinch tried to steal Christmas by taking all the presents and Christmas decorations from the town of Who-ville, and when he left, it was clean as a whistle. But the Grinch couldn't actually steal Christmas, because Christmas is a spirit, and you can't steal a spirit. Even though the Grinch had taken everyone's presents, joyful sounds still filled the air on Christmas morning in Who-ville. Why? Because all the little Who's in the town were celebrating the birth of Jesus.

It is very easy and very natural to be excited about the presents you received from your parents, but these old Christmas gifts are a reminder that in a few years even your new games and toys will find their way to the back of the closet or be thrown away. You may grow too old for them, or they may simply wear out.

But what about that other gift—the gift behind all the gifts we receive? This is the *love* of God, which gave us Jesus Christ, and the *love* of your parents, which gave you life. If anything is going to last, it will be the gift of love which is given day after day after day. That, of course, is the essence of the Christmas spirit. It is also the reason that the Grinch, mean as he was, could not steal the joy of Who-ville.

I truly hope that the spirit of Christmas will last for you. And I think it will, because every Sunday we celebrate God's great gift of Jesus. You may never have thought of Sunday in this way before. But every Sunday is like Christmas Day, when we open and give thanks for the gift of God's love, Jesus Christ.

May the spirit of Christmas be with you today, tomorrow, and every day to come.

My One-Tenth Box

Text: Genesis 28:18-22
Appropriate Day: Stewardship Sunday, any Sunday
Summary: Just as we budget money for our needs and wishes, we should set aside one-tenth of what we have for God.
Props: A box with a removable top—e.g., a popcorn container; some change

This morning I came prepared with my one-tenth box. What is a one-tenth box, you ask? I'll be happy to explain it to you.

When I was growing up, my parents kept a lot of boxes in a drawer. And every week when my father got paid, they would put a certain amount of money in each box. There was a box marked "clothing," a box marked "food," a box marked "housing," another box labeled "entertainment," and one last box marked "1/10." (Have a card marked with this fraction so that younger children can visual one-tenth in their minds.)

I thought I understood how my parents used the other boxes, but curiosity finally drove me to ask my parents about the one-tenth box. They explained to me that they used the boxes to budget their money each week so that they didn't spend so much on one need that they had nothing left for a different need. But the one-tenth box was different, because it wasn't meant to pay any of the family bills or provide us with money to see a movie or eat in a restaurant. Instead, it was God's share. The money in that box belonged to God, and each week we emptied the box and brought the money to church to be put into the offering.

In a minute I'm going to explain how you figure what a tenth of your allowance is. But first it's important that you know that the idea of a one-tenth box was not my parents'—it wasn't even the Church's idea. It's an idea that's even older than the Church itself, because it's mentioned in the Old Testament long before we read about the birth of Jesus and the beginning of the Christian Church. We know about the ten commandments that God gave to Moses. And we should also know about Jacob's promise to return to God one-tenth of what he had. It was something like a pledge on Jacob's part. If God would be with him and give him bread to eat and clothing to wear, Jacob would gladly return to God a tenth of what he had freely received from Him.

And now we must learn how to figure what a tenth is. I came prepared this morning with some change. (Ten pennies and twenty dimes work well in examples.) If your parents gave you ten pennies, a tenth of that would be one penny; if they gave you ten dimes or a dollar, a tenth would be one dime; and if they gave you two dollars, a tenth would be two dimes. (Illustrate your figuring with the pennies and dimes while you're talking.) Who can tell me what a tenth of three dollars would be? (Solicit some answers.) Now you have the idea: you take the total and divide by ten, or figure a dime for every dollar of your allowance.

My parents taught me an important lesson with their labeled boxes. They knew, as I know now, that unless you have some place to set your money aside, it's going to get spent. And we must also remember to set aside the Lord's one-tenth even if we haven't been to worship.

As you can see, this sermon is not going to be finished when you leave for your Sunday school classes. You and your parents should discuss what an appropriate allowance would be for someone your age. And I hope that they'll help you make a one-tenth box, because Jacob's pledge is just like one of the ten commandments. We need to practice it all the time.

Note: This sermon illustrates another way to leave the conclusion open-ended, allowing the listener to complete the message. Jesus' encounter with the rich man who asks about eternal life ends in a similar fashion (Luke 18:18-23).

Adding a Drop of Love

Text: Luke 21:1-4
Appropriate Day: The first Sunday of Lent or One Great Hour of Sharing
Summary: Take a few pennies, and add a drop of love—it can make a difference.
Props: An offering box; a clear bowl (e.g., a punch bowl) filled with water, an eye dropper, red food coloring, and two grain bags (available at hardware stores)—one full, labeled "U.S.A.," the other half empty

As part of my welcome this morning, I mentioned that this is the first Sunday of Lent. Lent is that period of forty days during which we prepare ourselves for Easter. And one of the ways this church prepares itself is with a special offering known as One Great Hour of Sharing. I have always liked that name because it has such a nice ring to it: as Christians we unite to help others in that special time, that "one great hour of sharing." You'll be getting a head start on the rest of us, because as you leave your Sunday school classes this morning, each of you will receive an offering box that looks like this one. (Hold up box.) Then, on the last Sunday in March, you and all of us will bring our offering to church in order to celebrate the One Great Hour of Sharing.

On my left and on my right are two grain bags. I brought these here today because they are signs that help us better understand why we take this special offering during Lent. This bag is full, and it has on it the letters "U.S.A.," which stand for

76

"the United States of America." And it's full because we who live in American and in _____, _____ (name your city and state) have a "full bag" of just about everything—food, clothing, housing, tools, grain, hospitals. The other bag is not even half full. It stands for the many people and many countries whose bag is almost empty of just about everything—food, clothing, housing, tools, grain, hospitals.

One Great Hour of Sharing is how we as Christians take some from our full bag and begin to fill this empty bag. And on _____ (supply the date) we will do just that: we will take your offering boxes and put them into this bag and see if we can't fill it up.

During the next few weeks you will be dropping coins into our box, and many of those coins will be pennies. You might think that a few pennies or even a few dimes can't make much difference when there are so many needy people in the world, and when their needs are so great. It takes a lot of money to build a hospital or train a doctor. But I hope you will never believe that your offering, no matter how small, doesn't count.* Let's not forget that there are thousands—even millions—of Protestant Christians who will join us in this offering.

But even more important is the fact that as Christians we add something extra—God's love. With every penny or dollar, we mix in a little of God's love, just as the widow did when she gave her last penny. Not only does the Church bring food and medicine and trained men and women to help those needy people; it also brings the Good News of God's love. And when people are hungry, lonely, scared, and hopeless, they really need to know that they are loved.

One drop of love, like one penny, doesn't seem like much. But let me show you that it can make a difference. How many drops of water would you say are in this punch bowl? (Solicit several answers.) A thousand million. That's a good guess, and since I didn't count the drops, I'm going to take your word for

*The Fellowship of the Least Coin, an international fellowship of women based upon the story of the widow's mite, is an interesting example of this belief. Keep in mind that a sequel sermon could be based on this story (Luke 21:1-4), in which the penny becomes the "drop of love." This story is itself a dramatic demonstration, so be creative; use your imagination.

it. And to this bowl of a thousand million drops of water I'm going to add just *one* drop of red food coloring—red because that's the color of love. When I add the drop and stir the water, that one drop colors the entire bowl of water.

Take a few pennies here and a few pennies there and add a few drops of love or even one drop of love—and it can make a difference. Believe me! Believe yourself! It can make a difference.

Note: The inspiration for this sermon came from a prayer by Helen Kromer in *For Heaven's Sake*, quoted by Jo Carr and Imogene Sorley in *Bless This Mess & Other Prayers:*

> A drop in the bucket
> Is only a drop—
> A minor and moist detail;
> For a drop can't change
> The color and taste
> In a ten-quart watering pail.

> But if the drop
> Has the color of love
> And the taste of tears divine,
> One drop dropped into
> The vessel of life
> Can turn the water to wine. Amen.

Breakfast of Champions

Text: Luke 2:52 (the Good News Bible): "Jesus grew both in body and in wisdom, gaining favor with God and men."
Season: Any
Summary: Part of growing up is to understand that dreams of being champions can prevent us from maturing as "complete" Christians.
Props: A box of Wheaties

I'm putting in front of you a box that's a familiar sight at many breakfast tables. But it's not just any old box of cereal—it's "the breakfast of champions." At least when I was growing up the ads led us to believe that every champion began the morning with a bowl of Wheaties. On the front or back of the box there was always a picture of a superstar who had set a new world's record in a sport like running, jumping, or swimming.

We all have dreams of becoming some kind of champion—a champion soccer player, a champion chess player, a champion piano player, or a champion mathematician. We all have a deep, burning desire to be the *best*, or if not the best there is, at least the best among our friends.

I once knew a boy who thought that if ate enough Wheaties and trained very hard, he could become a great football player. But it wasn't to be. As he grew older, his body scarcely grew at all. And the other football players—well, they kept getting bigger and stronger. By the time this young man was a freshman in college, he was the smallest player on the team. It was a hard decision for him to make, but the next year he chose not to play football at all for the first time in many, many years. When he did that, he gave up his dream of being a great football player. But he also discovered that he had a lot more time to develop some of his other abilities and talents.

What am I trying to say to you? Am I telling you to give up your dreams of being a champion? No! Dreams are important and valuable because they make us set goals for ourselves—goals that make us work harder to become the very best we can be in a particular sport or activity. But our dreams of being champions can easily become so important that everything else becomes unimportant. And as a consequence we don't grow up in all the ways that Christians should.

We do not know much about Jesus as a young boy. But in the Gospel of Luke we do read that Jesus grew up in different ways. Luke tells us that Jesus grew big and strong, which says something about how he developed physically. He also grew in wisdom and understanding, which means Jesus learned about the meaning of life from the Bible and other books, and from people. And, thirdly, Luke writes that Jesus grew in favor with God, which means that it was important whether or not he obeyed God. In other words, Jesus grew in many ways in order to become a complete person and a complete Christian.

That boy who didn't become a great football player was me. And as you can see, I did find something to do with my life besides play football. I still like my Wheaties with fruit. And I still like to play football and dream. But I no longer believe being a champion is the most important thing in my life. I'm content just keeping my body healthy and in good shape, and trying hard to continue to grow in wisdom and in favor with God.

I feel like offering a prayer to God. Will you join me? "Dear Lord, we give thanks that we are forever changing and growing. Bless us as we make our dreams of being champions include the joy of learning to be Christians—the best Christians we can possibly be. Amen."

DRAMATIC PARTICIPATION

Given in the tradition of the parable, these sermons require the listeners' actual participation in the drama.

Building a Church

Text: I Corinthians 3:5-11
Appropriate Day: Worldwide Communion Sunday, any Sunday
Summary: The Church is all kinds of people joined together, with Christ as its center.
Props: A hand-held mirror, a paper bag containing several different hats, and a cross

Everyone here knows what a church looks like. Would someone like to give me a description of a church? (If the children who answer describe a building, remind them that they are giving descriptions of a building, not a congregation. You may offer to show them a picture of a church by holding up a hand mirror and letting them see their own reflection.)

Some of you may even know a little song that does a good job of describing a church. It goes like this:

> The church is not a building,
> The church is not a steeple,
> The church is not a resting place,
> The church is a people!

I thought it would be fun if we could build a church this morning, and a very special church at that, because we want to build the Church as it includes people all over the world—the universal Church. Let's begin to build this "people church" by imagining who its members would be. As you think of different people who might belong to it, I'll ask you to come

82

forward, describe the church member you're thinking of, and start forming a line. Just to give you a few ideas, I've brought in my bag of different hats. The first one is an Indian headband—an important hat, because we easily forget that there are Christian Indians who belong to the Church. (Come prepared with other hats, such as a king's crown, a farmer's hat, a coolie hat, a sombrero, etc. For other original ideas, use a Magic Marker to decorate plain hats made of cardboard. Solicit a variety of answers from the children before continuing.)

Our church looks like it's complete, because it includes many different people, but something still isn't right. Everyone is standing in a line, but the Church is people who are doing exciting things. We need our church to be IN ACTION. (Have children form action poses in which they are touching each other.) And if the Church is going to be a true church, we must make one other change. We need a foundation, a center, and that center is Jesus Christ. If we can all form a circle, I will put this cross in the center to symbolize the presence of Jesus Christ.

At last, our church is built. And I'd like everyone in the congregation to take a mental picture of what you see. A better-built church you will not see for a long time.

Note: In this sermon the listener-participant *carries* away with him a *picture* of the sermon. It is, therefore, "portable" and picturable—two ingredients for an effective sermon.

An Apple a Day

Text: Genesis 1:31
Season: Fall
Summary: To truly experience God's created world is to give thanks.
Props: One very red, delicious-looking apple, plus an apple for each child.*

Somehow the first apple of the season tastes the best. And the last apple, after we have had lots and lots of apples, doesn't taste nearly as good. Personally, I also enjoy much more the apples I pick myself. Not only is it fun to go to an orchard and see where the apples are growing; you have the advantage of picking the apples that look the best to you. And of all the apples I saw when I went to the orchard last Saturday, this one looked especially delicious. I'm going to put it aside for the moment. But while I was picking, I also had you in mind, so I've brought along an apple for each of you. (Distribute apples.) You may eat it, but I'm going to ask that you eat it in a very special way this morning.

First, I want you to hold the apple in your hands and polish it by rubbing it—give it a good shine. While you're doing this, feel it with your fingertips. Does it feel like anything else, or does it feel like only an apple can feel?

Now that you've polished your apple, hold it up to the light and look at its color. You'll discover that your apple is actually

*Raisins, peanuts, or other seasonal foods would also work well.

many different colors—not just red. How many different colors can you count? Are the colors unique to an apple?

We have felt the beauty of an apple through our fingertips, and seen it with our eyes. What about our ears? Let's listen to an apple. It's simple to do. Just take a small bite and strain your ears to catch every sound that's made as you sink your teeth into the skin of your apple. Is it a sound you have heard before? Describe the sound to yourself.

I'm wondering if any of you have taken the time to smell your apple. (Children can do this while they are chewing the bite they've taken—which will take a while!) Go ahead: give the apple a good sniff. This will be a test of how good your sense of smell is. Is it like any other smell? Can you describe it?

Finally, we use our last sense—that of taste. Close your eyes this time, take a small bite, and chew it slowly. Is your apple sweet or sour or a delicate balance of both? Keep your eyes closed and enjoy your bite as much as you can.

(Turning to the congregation): I'm sorry I didn't have an apple for each of you. But I'll bet this was the best apple you've ever tasted.

When God finished creating the world, according to the book of Genesis, "he saw everything that he had made, and behold, it was very good." We don't realize *how* good until we take the time to discover the fullness of the beauty of each individual thing. I'm going to take this single apple I've been saving and place it on the communion table now. It will be part of my offering this morning. Let us give thanks, in prayer, as part of our offering:

"Dear God—wonderful Creator—we thank you for the beauty of just one apple: for its feel, its color, its smell, its sound, and its taste. Give us lots of apples, God, but let us still marvel at the beauty of just one apple. Amen."

All the Glue in the World

Text: Genesis 1:31
Appropriate Day or Season: Spring, Earth Day
Summary: There is evidence of God's creating hand all around us. Let us wonder at and preserve what God has created.
Props: A flower. My favorite is Queen Anne's lace. Very common, it is often considered a weed but is actually a wild carrot. Take time to tell how it got its name: it looks like the lace worn by queens. A beautiful rose or a crocus is also effective.

Preparation: Begin by asking for two volunteers, one younger and one older. Tell the younger child he has the easier task. Let him tear the flower into little pieces and put them into the cupped hands of the older child. Then turn to the older child and tell her that she has the more difficult task. Ask her to put the flower back together just as it was. After she gets over her shock, ask her if she could put the flower back if you gave her an hour, a whole day, a month. Ask her if any person in the world could help her restore the flower to its original beauty. Finally, ask her if she could accomplish the task if she had all the glue in the world.

Take the pieces of the flower in your hands. As you are dropping the pieces onto the floor, say something like what follows below.

I wonder why it is that we are able to build spaceships that travel to the moon and back, but we cannot put a little flower back together again, not even with all the glue in the world? Could the reason be that *we* built the spaceship, but *God* gave us this flower? And God has not only given us this flower; he has created many, many tokens of his love that we cannot put back after we have destroyed them.*

I would ask that you enjoy the springtime: take walks, listen and look at all of God's beauty that surrounds you. But please don't destroy anything you can't recreate.

Note: This sermon has other possible endings. For an older group the emphasis could be a demonstration that, at our very best, we as builders and inventors are only imitators of God's creativity. In either case, the sermon is a subtle proof of God's existence, but I would avoid making this aspect explicit. Why? Because explicit proofs only challenge the child/youth to argue about God rather than give thanks for the signs of God's creating power.

*Father Michael Quoist's popular book, entitled *Prayers*, is dedicated to the theology that "if we knew how to look at life through God's eyes, we would see it as innumerable tokens of the love of the Creator seeking the love of his creatures."

Yesterday I Stomped on a Frog

Text: Isaiah 42:5; Exodus 20:13; Genesis 1:24
Season: Any
Summary: We should make a conscious commitment not to kill another living thing.
Props: A bell that a child can ring—e.g., a dinner bell

Some of you may have heard of Albert Schweitzer. He was born in Germany about a hundred years ago, a famous man with many talents: he was a marvelous organist, a gifted preacher, and a New Testament scholar. (I even read a few of his books during my training to become a minister.) Yet, in spite of his accomplishments, Albert Schweitzer was still not convinced that he was doing enough with his life, so he decided to return to medical school and become a doctor. His dream was to become a medical missionary—and he did. He was well known for his work in Africa, where he built a famous hospital in a place called Lambarene.

When he was about eight years old, Albert Schweitzer had a very unusual experience. He was out playing one day when some friends asked him to join them; they were going to shoot birds with their slingshots. At first Albert didn't want to go, but after repeated pleading he gave in. Creeping up behind a rock, Albert took aim to shoot a songbird, but just then he heard a church bell ringing. It was, in Albert's own words, like a voice from heaven. He threw down his slingshot, horrified at the thought of having come so close to killing a harmless creature. And in that moment there was born in Schweitzer's heart what would become one of the great ideas of modern man: reverence or respect for life.

I have here a bell, and in a minute I'm going to invite you to come forward and ring it. And as you ring it, you must pledge to try not to hurt another living thing.

But you may be saying to yourself, "I don't know if I can keep that pledge." Let me tell you another short story about a six-year-old boy who refused to ring the bell.* After considerable urging, and with downcast eyes, he explained, "I don't believe I deserve to ring the bell, because yesterday I stomped on a frog." The important thing to remember is that you're going *to try* not to hurt another living thing. Maybe you won't always be able to keep your promise, but if you're willing to try, I invite you to come forward and ring this bell.

Note: Later I wondered why I didn't use the bell in the church belfry. That would certainly be more dramatic, and would give the children the chance to decide, out of public view, if they really want to ring the bell. (They could do this after Sunday school.)

Bear in mind the learning pyramid (Part I, p. 16)—the act of ringing would reinforce the verbal story. The church bell might then become a symbol to the children, because every time they heard the bell ring (or rung it themselves), they would remember the story of Albert Schweitzer and would mentally participate in the story's re-enactment.

*In the Albert Schweitzer Friendship House, founded by Mrs. Erica Anderson just outside Great Barrington, Massachusetts, there is a tower in which hangs a bell with a long rope. Here children are invited to make their pledge after they have seen a moving film (made by Mrs. Anderson) about the last years of Dr. Schweitzer's life.

Fifty-Two Card Pick-Up

Text: John 13:1-11
Appropriate Time: Easter week*
Summary: Jesus gave us specific examples (demonstra-
tions) of what it means to serve one another, one of which
was washing the feet of his disciples.
Props: A deck of cards

*Preparation: Spend a few minutes reviewing the
events leading up to Good Friday.*

As a minister I am always trying to relate what happened long
ago to some experience with which you are familiar. I know a
game that will help us understand what happened when Jesus
and his disciples celebrated their last meal together.

I'll need a volunteer to play this game with me, which is a
very simple card game. (Show the cards as you choose a child
to work with.) Are you ready? The game is called fifty-two
card pick-up. I start it by doing this (fanning the cards all over
the chancel), and you finish it by picking the cards up.

(Wait until the child has picked up one or two cards.)
"Jim" (address the child), I really believe you would pick up all
the cards, and some of your friends would probably help you.
But I suspect that if I were your brother or sister or someone

---

*A different text for this sermon could be Jesus' command about forgetting
ourselves and carrying our cross (Mark 8:34-38). This would be an appropriate
message for Halloween or April Fools' Day, because the accent would be upon a
trick that becomes an example.

your age, you would tell me why I should pick the cards up, and why that was a rotten trick to play on you. But because I'm older than you, and your minister, and because this happened in worship on Sunday morning, you would probably pick up all the cards and give them back to me. What I want you to do, though, is sit here on the top chancel step while *I* pick up all the rest of the cards. (As you are picking up the cards, pause every now and then and tell the story of John 13. Explain how Jesus poured water into a basin and one by one washed the feet of his disciples, and explain how Peter protested.)

Jesus washed his disciples' feet because he wanted to give them a visible demonstration of what it means to serve others even if you don't have to. (I have in mind Martin Luther's statement: "A Christian is the most free lord of all, subject to none; a Christian is the most dutiful servant of all, subject to everyone.") And so I give to you this visible demonstration of my love for each of you, and my willingness to be your servant.

Note: As in Jesus' use of parable actions such as the washing, the proclamation is the action, not the words. Any further explanation cuts off the process necessary for the individual to remember the image you have created, and prevents it from freely playing itself out in his or her life.

What to Do with a Chocolate Chip Cookie?

Text: Isaiah 58:6-10; Matthew 25:35
Season: Any
Summary: Whether or not we will share what we have with others is a decision each of us must consciously make.
Props: Several oversized chocolate chip cookies; several construction-paper-and-string signs, printed with the names of both well-to-do and poor countries, that children can hang around their necks

With a few words of introduction, read the passage from Isaiah. Then divide the children into groups of about five to ten (ideally three to four groups). Give each group a sign, a few printed with the names of prosperous countries, the others printed with the names of poor countries. Next explain to the children, "Today we're going to play a game—a very serious game, though. Some of you will represent countries with plenty of food, and others will represent countries with very little food."

Now give a cookie to each representative of the prosperous countries, and tell the children representing the poor countries that they get nothing. (Don't give cookies to very young children. Give them only to children who can act as leaders of their groups.) Say nothing more (don't over-explain or lead); just wait. Depending upon what happens—and especially if nothing happens—you might say to the representatives, "You have a few minutes to decide what to do with your cookies."

The conclusion must be ad-libbed. Most likely the

representatives of the prosperous countries will give away some of the cookies to friends who then might share with others.

When the distribution is complete, summarize the experience by recalling the Scripture passage. You might conclude with these words: "Jesus said to his friends, 'When I have gone away and you try to find me, you will see me in the eyes of every man, woman, and child who stands hungry.'"*

*Mahatma Gandhi once said, "To millions who have to go without two meals a day, the only acceptable form in which God dare appear is food."

THE PANTOMIME
AND THE ECHO

These sermons require the listeners to process non-verbal clues and use their imaginations.

The Good Samaritan* (Part I)

Text: Luke 10:25-37
Season: Any
Summary: God's love makes it possible for anyone to be a good Samaritan.

Introduction: One day Jesus was tested with this question: "If I am supposed to love my neighbor as myself, who is my neighbor?" Jesus answered by telling a story—this story. I ask that you pay attention because I'll be telling the story again and asking you to join me by being an echo.

I am who I am (point to yourself).
One day I put on my sandals (pretend to put on sandals),
And my traveling cloak (mimic slipping arms into loose cloak).
I took my money bag (hold imaginary bag in fist),
And hid it in my belt (mimic tucking it in wide belt).
Then I started on my way (walk in place)
From Jerusalem to Jericho (sweep arm in wide arc),
Uphill and downhill (lean backward, lean forward),
Past dark caves where robbers might hide (look fearful).
I pretended I wasn't afraid (stand straight, hands clasped
   behind back);
But all of a sudden I was surrounded by robbers (arms go up),

*Adapted from "Living the Word," Level 4 (Winter 1979-1980), JED curriculum.

And one of them hit me (crouch as if to protect self);
That was the last thing I remember (bend further down).
After a while (cup hand to ear),
I heard footsteps (cross arms, slapping hands on arms).
The footsteps grew louder (slap more loudly).
It was a priest (stop slapping; hold arms akimbo).
He said, "Can't stop now, sonny" (look down and shake head),
"But I'll come back later" (wave good-bye).
After a while (cup hand to ear),
I heard new footsteps (raise hands to shoulder level; snap
    fingers).
It was a Levite (continue snapping fingers).
He said, "Too bad, too bad" (shake head);
Then he went on his way (wave good-bye).
Soon I heard other footsteps (slap thighs, one after the other).
It was a Samaritan on a donkey (continue thigh-slapping).
"Whoa! Need any help?" (mimic pulling reins, lean over and
    look down);
Then he jumped down (jump up and down once),
And took off his cloak (mimic taking off cloak),
Tore it into strips (pretend to tear strips of cloth),
And bandaged my wounds (mimic rolling bandages on
    wounded areas).
He lifted me onto his donkey (mimic lifting and placing body
    gently),
And slowly we went on our way (slap thighs more slowly),
Until we came to an inn (mimic pulling back on reins).
He carried me inside (arms outstretched in carrying position),
And laid me on a bed (pretend to place body on bed).
"Here is some money," he said to the innkeeper (mimic taking
    coins from bag);
"I will pay all that is owed." (pretend to tuck money bag back
    in belt).
Then he went on his way (slap thighs).

Now I ask you (point finger at listeners),
Which one loved me as a neighbor (point as if to three distinct
    persons):

The priest who said, "Can't stop now, sonny"? (hold arms
    akimbo);
The Levite who said, "Too bad, too bad"? (snap fingers once);
Or the Good Samaritan? (slap hands on thigh).
Go thou (point to one side of congregation),
And do likewise (swing arm to other side of congregation).

The Good Samaritan, Echo Style (Part II): The Loving Warlock*

Introduction: This time we'll retell the story of the Good Samaritan as Jesus might have told it to us. You now have a feeling for the way the story will be told. So be my echo and repeat the same words and actions after me.

I am who I am (point to yourself).
One day I put on my shoes (pretend to put on shoes),
And my overcoat (mimic slipping arms into coat).
I took my money (open hand)
And hid it in my jeans pocket (slip hand into back pocket).
Then I got on my ten-speed racer (imitate climbing on bike),
And started on my way (walk in place)
From _____ to _____ (name two local communities;
    walk in place),
Uphill and downhill (lean forward; lean backward),
Past big trees where muggers might hide (look fearful).
I pretended I wasn't afraid (stand straight, hands clasped
    behind back).
But all of a sudden (arms go up),
Muggers jumped out at me! (crouch as if to protect self).
One of them hit me (kneel, head down);
That was the last thing I remember (bend further down).
After a while (cup hand to ear)

*The Warlocks are a motorcycle gang in the city where I used to live. You may have to substitute a name that children in your church would recognize.

I heard footsteps (cross arms, slapping hands on arms).

The footsteps became louder (slap more loudly).

It was one of the local ministers (stop slapping; hold arms akimbo).

He said, "Can't stop now, sonny" (look down and shake head),

"But I'll come back later" (wave good-bye).

After a while (cup hand to ear),

I heard new footsteps (raise hands to shoulder level, snap fingers).

It was a local schoolteacher (continue snapping fingers).

She said, "Too bad, too bad" (shake head);

Then she went on her way (wave good-bye).

Soon I heard the sound of a motorcycle (make sound of engine).

It was a tough-looking Warlock (or use name of any local motorcycle gang; hold thumbs up).

He said, "Hey, need any help?" (lean over and look down).

Then he jumped down (jump up and down once),

And tore off his leather jacket (pretend to take off coat),

And wrapped it around me (move hands in circular wrapping motion).

Then he lifted me onto his motorcycle (mimic lifting and placing body gently),

And we went slowly on our way (hold hands as if gripping handlebars, make sound of engine).

Soon we came to a Holiday Inn (make sound of screeching brakes).

He carried me inside (arms outstretched in carrying position),

Laid me on a bed (pretend to place body on bed),

And paid the manager twenty dollars (mimic handing out a few bills).

"Take care of my buddy," he said (one hand outstretched, palm up).

"I'll take care of the cost" (pat back pocket where money would be).

Then this kind Warlock went on his way (hold hands as if gripping handlebars).

Now I ask you (point finger at audience),

Which one loved me as a Christian (point to three imaginary people):

The minister who said, "Can't stop now"? (hold arms akimbo);

The schoolteacher who said, "Too bad, too bad"? (snap fingers once);

Or the Warlock? (hold hands as if gripping handlebars, make sound of engine).

Go thou (point to one side of audience),

And do likewise (sweeping motion to the other side).

Note: The parable of the Good Samaritan is ripe with exegetical problems, but it is sufficient to note that it has two themes. There is first the theme of what it means to be a good neighbor. If this had been the story's only purpose, it would have been far better if the wounded man had been the Samaritan, because it would have more perfectly illustrated that Christian love has no limits (i.e., it includes one's enemies). But when the half-breed Samaritan becomes the compassionate one, rather than the three Jewish passers-by, then the parable is about reversal and judgment; it is a story not so much about doing a good deed (cf. II Chron. 28:1-15) as about the inbreaking of the Kingdom that reverses our expectations about *who* can be good.

For this reason I've chosen to tell the story twice. The first version emphasizes the theme of being a good neighbor ("Go thou and do likewise"), and the second highlights the embarrassing realization of who was the good neighbor (Which of these three, do you think, proved neighbor to the man who fell among the robbers?). The story's point is that we must decide, based upon our particular situation, who might be the least likely to hear the Gospel, and respond with Christian compassion.

Read as a story, "The Good Samaritan" is a model of what it means to be a good neighbor; told as a parable, it invites us to abandon our usual way of behaving by *reversing* our perception of the way things always seem to be.

Overcoming Temptation

Text: Exodus 20 (eighth and tenth commandments)
Season: Any
Summary: The way to overcome temptation is by praying and turning our backs on the thing we desire.
Props: A table and chair; you in the traditional white face of the mime, if you choose to apply it.

Today I'm going to tell a story through pantomime, which is a story without words. And because the words are missing, we gain a better sense of the inner feelings of the actor. This particular pantomime is about three words: "steal," "covet," and "temptation." According to the eighth commandment, we should not steal what belongs to another person, and according to the tenth commandment, we should not covet or desire with our heart what belongs to another. And temptation is that feeling, that impulse, that ever-present itch to disobey God.

Scene I: *You shall not steal.* (Announce this.)
Begin by playing a game with yourself at the table (e.g., ball and jacks, cards).
Suddenly, your eyes fall upon something you want, and you begin to grin.
You walk around this object, and your grin becomes wider.
You look to see if you are being watched.
You quickly grab the object and run back to your table and chair.
You put the object on the table, staring at it and grinning.

102

Gradually, your stare changes, and your grin is not so wide.
No matter what you do or where you move, that object
reminds you of your disobedience. Your grin disappears.

Scene II: *You shall not covet.* (Announce this.)
You are playing the same game.
As your eyes wander, they're attracted to something.
Your whole body is attracted to this object (or person), and
you begin to grin.
You circle it, and your hands reach out and almost grab it.
Your smile gets bigger.
You return to your table and chair, but all the time you look
over your shoulder and grin.
No matter what you do or where you move, your eyes still
return to the thing you desire.
Sitting in your chair, you are transfixed by this object. Your
grin slowly turns to despair.
(You may wish to stop the pantomime here and ask the children what they felt and learned and how they would explain
the difference between stealing and coveting: e.g., coveting is
stealing with one's heart. If we were to be satisfied with being
good teachers, we might say "well done" and conclude this sermon. But since we are also preachers of the Good News, we
present a third scene which illumines the grace God gives us to
overcome temptation.)

Scene 3: *Overcoming temptation* (Announce this.)
You are playing the same game.
As your eyes wander, they are attracted to something.
You get up and begin circling this object, grinning.
Your hands shake, and your body trembles with desire.
Using your will, you turn your back on the object and begin
walking away.
As you walk, your head and body begin to turn back to the
object, but you control them.
You feel the pull of the object so strongly that you have to hold
your head with your hands to keep it from turning toward
the object.
You stop and offer a prayer.
You reach your table and sit down.

You realize that the desire to look is no longer so strong.
You are able to return to your game and smile without being
concerned with the object. You have forgotten it.

Love Conquers All

Text: Romans 12:17-21 or Luke 23:33-34
Appropriate Day or Season: Easter; any Sunday
Summary: Forgiveness is that kind of Christian love which
can overcome hate.
Props: Five or more helium-filled balloons (one, which may
be larger than the others, has a cross on it); a large pin; five
or more actors (in the traditional white face of the mime, if
you like); a piano player

Begin by reading the Scripture passage.

The pantomime is this: The first actor comes dancing down the
aisle holding the largest balloon. Her joy is obvious as she
moves about the chancel. She pauses to trace the cross on her
balloon. To the sound of light, joyful music, others come dancing down the aisles, but without balloons. When the first actor
sees that they are without balloons, she goes to one side of the
chancel where a handful of balloons hang (more if they are to
be given later to the congregation). She then gives each mime a
balloon. Their smiles grow bigger when they receive this gift.
Note: It is important, here, that the mimes express joy in the
giving and receiving of the balloons and not in their possession.
To symbolize this, they might also exchange balloons. The
balloon with the cross ends up with the first actor.

The music now changes from joyful praise to melodrama;
although no one knows it, the villain is hiding behind the
pulpit. He subtly appears and gradually approaches the first

mime. As the other actors become aware of his approach, they back away. Then, with his hatpin poised high, the villain strikes and breaks the balloon with the cross. With the exception of the villain, everyone is sad. They bow their heads and pull down their balloons. The music becomes dirge-like.

At first hesitant and doubtful, the actor closest to the first mime hands her a balloon. (She may choose to draw a cross on her balloon as she did before, but it is not necessary.) Gradually joy returns as the mimes trade balloons; the music changes, too.

The villain looks disconcerted, even angry. All the actors again back away, leaving only the villain and the first mime center-stage on the chancel. She notices the dejection of the villain, and, after thoughtful consideration, she gives her balloon to him. At first he refuses it, but then changes his mind. Now all the actors begin to return to the chancel, and several offer their balloon to the first mime. The music now becomes victorious.

The pantomime can end in a variety of ways. The mimes might give balloons to the congregation. Our choice was to ask the congregation to join in the singing of "Pass It On" by Kurt Kaiser.

Note: Because a pantomime is wordless, the pictures painted by the actors become amplified, and are crucial. Thus the mimes should freeze their significant poses for two to four seconds so they can "set." The observers become active participants because they must supply the narrative to match the action—hence the power of pantomime. The symbolism in this sermon isn't necessary; it's added so that the pantomime can operate at several levels simultaneously (see "Targeting the Sermon" in Part I).

THE STORY

These sermons have a well-defined plot and characters. (This form is one of the most difficult to use successfully; the previously explored forms should probably be mastered first.)

Looking for the Devil

Text: Ephesians 6:13; Proverbs 8:13
Season: Any
Summary: The evil we seek to cast out is the evil we find in ourselves.
Props: A good picture of the Devil*

Today I've brought along a picture of someone everyone will recognize, and yet I'll bet that no one has ever seen this person. (Show the picture and wait for responses.) It seems that I was right on both counts. Everyone knew this was a picture of the Devil even though no one has actually ever seen him. It makes me wonder if we would really know the Devil if we met him or her or it.

One day, when I was a little boy, I crawled out of bed and went looking for the Devil. And where do you think I found him? I didn't find him in a hole. And I didn't find him in a dark corner. I didn't find a mean-looking monster, red all over with a pitchfork tail. In fact, I didn't find anything I could grab and shake and tell to get out of my life. I wonder why I didn't find the Devil when I went looking for him?

You know what I think? When I was a young child I didn't look in the right place—I forgot to look inside myself. Now that I'm older I believe the Devil is actually all the evil in the world that is in all of us. The Devil can be the little voice in us

---

*Valerie Stalder's *Even the Devil Is Afraid of a Shrew* contains some marvelous pictures of a devil.

that tempts us to say mean things and to do things that hurt other people.

Have you ever said to yourself, "I know I shouldn't be doing this, but I'm going to do it anyway"? And when you get caught or you think about the awful thing you did, you say to yourself, "Gee, I wish I hadn't done that." That, my friends, is how evil works, and how it stays alive.

The day I went looking for the Devil and found him inside my heart, I also discovered that I could chase him out, because I found that God's spirit also lives in my heart. And I discovered something even more amazing: that when there is love in my heart, there is no room left for evil to trouble me. So whenever I'm tempted to be mean or unkind, I just think about how God loves me and looks after me, and in no time at all my evil thoughts are gone.

It's not very often that I write a poem, but here's one that fits the occasion:

> The Day I Went Looking for the Devil
>
> I didn't find the Devil in a deep, dark hole,
> And I didn't find him spying from a big high pole;
> Instead I found him talking in whispers to me,
> Saying how much fun being mean would be.
> But thanks be to God, I found a great art,
> A way to get the Devil out of my heart:
> I think a kind thought, I do a good deed,
> And evil goes down to death and defeat.

Note: It's important that we don't end sermons on a negative (imperative) note; we need to offer a positive (indicative) possibility. Compare this sermon with Scene III of the pantomime "Overcoming Temptation."

Let's resolve to double our efforts to underscore the *power* of the Gospel to lift us out of our usual condition. Because we are so good at describing the human predicament, we often neglect to demonstrate the new things possible in Christ.

The Story of Tom Gobble

Text: I Chronicles 16:34; Psalm 145:10-13
Appropriate Day: Thanksgiving
Props: A flannel board, and pictures of a small turkey and a big turkey

Preparation: Begin by briefly describing what the word "greedy" means—i.e., "to grab."

Tom was the smallest turkey in Farmer Jones' barnyard (put his picture up), but Tom was a very greedy little turkey. At night he was always the first one in the barn so that he could get the best bed. In the morning he was always the first one out the door so that he could be the first to clean himself in the bath. And at mealtime he was always the first to gobble up the food. Tom Gobble was a sight to see when it was time to eat: he would spread his feathers and run through the barnyard, screaming, "Gobble, gobble, gobble, you better get out of my way!" As days turned into months and Tom continued his greedy ways, he grew bigger and bigger and bigger, until one day he was the biggest turkey in the barnyard (change pictures).

Because Thanksgiving Day was coming, Farmer Jones was sizing up his turkeys to see which one would make the best Thanksgiving dinner. Well, you can guess what happened. When Tom Gobble saw Farmer Jones coming after him, he wished he hadn't been so greedy—but his wishing had come too late. Farmer Jones fixed him for Thanksgiving dinner, and that afternoon all the barnyard animals began to sing this little song:

> O, Tom Gobble, you had to be so greedy,
> You got so fat, though once you were so spindly.
> Your big fat tummy caught the eye of Farmer Jones,
> And now you're just a pile of bones.

Of course, the story of Tom Gobble is not just a story about a turkey. It's a story about us, too, because we can also be pretty greedy at times. It seems that we always want to be first in line, to have the best seat or the biggest cookie; and at the dinner table our hands are a blur as we grab for the chicken or the rolls.

The opposite of being grabby or greedy is being thankful. In the Bible we read: "O give thanks to the Lord, for he is good; for his steadfast love endures for ever!"

Of course it's easy to be thankful at Thanksgiving time. But wouldn't it be great to be thankful each and every day? I have an idea. Are you willing to give it a try? Before our Thanksgiving dinner, we could ask God to help us be a little more thankful and a little less greedy. And—here is my idea—we could ask this not only on Thanksgiving Day but every day. The first thing we could do when we wake up in the morning is to offer a little prayer: "Dear God, I thank you for this day." It's really just as easy as it sounds—we only have to remember to do it. And I hope the story of Tom Gobble will help us to remember.

Note: In the story of Tom Gobble, the difference between being greedy and being thankful is a matter of life and death. But isn't it the same in the real world when thousands are dying of starvation every day? This is food for thought if we aim this sermon toward older children and young people.

Devils Are for Sale, Aren't They?

Text: Matthew 6:13 ("And lead us not into temptation . . ."); Mark 14:38
Season: Any
Summary: It is better to be busy for the Lord than idle for the Devil.
Props: Your best storytelling hat

Today I have a most intriguing story for you. I must admit that it's not my own story but one told many, many times by very wise men called Zen Masters.*

About two hundred years ago a gentleman who lived in a large house by the side of the road decided to go to the marketplace. As he was walking down a back street, he noticed a very unusual sight: a merchant stood beside a cage with a sign overhead which read: "Devil for sale." As he drew closer, the gentleman could see it was a yellow-skinned devil about the size of a large dog, with a tail and two long, sharp fangs. He sat quietly in his cage, gnawing on a bone.

After the gentleman regained his composure, he asked the merchant whether his devil was for sale. "Oh," said the merchant, "the devil isn't mine, but of course he is for sale. I want you to know this is an excellent devil—strong, hard-working, and able to do almost anything you ask of him. He knows how

*This story is adapted from Janwillem van de Wetering's *The Empty Mirror* (Boston: Houghton Mifflin, 1974), pp. 107-109. Even in its adapted form, this story is for older children and young people who are able to understand it as a pictorial representation of inner urges.

112

to cut firewood, clean house, wash dishes—he can even mend clothing. And my price isn't too high. If you give me two hundred dollars, he's yours."

The gentleman thought it was a fair price, so he paid the merchant and started on his way, carrying the devil in its cage.

"One moment," the merchant shouted. "Because you haven't bargained with me, I want to tell you something about this devil you ought to know. He is a devil, of course, and devils are no good. You know that, don't you?"

"Everyone knows that," the gentleman replied sharply. "Besides, you said he was an excellent devil."

"I did at that, and he will do everything I said he could do," replied the merchant. "I only wanted to warn you that you must keep him busy from sunup to sundown. If he has time to spare, time when he has nothing to do, then he's dangerous."

"If that's all," the gentleman said, "I will take my devil home and put him to work."

At first, everything went smoothly. Every morning the gentleman would call the devil, who bowed down obediently in front of him. The devil would then do everything the gentleman ordered him to do. If he wasn't working, he was playing or resting, but whatever he did, he was always obeying his master's orders.

Then, after some months, the gentleman met an old friend in the city, and because of the thrill of seeing his old acquaintance he forgot everything. He and his friend went to a cafe and started drinking to their friendship. Next they went to a nightclub where they had more drinks and spent the rest of the evening, having a grand time. The next morning the gentleman woke up in a strange place. At first he didn't know what had happened, but gradually it all came back to him. He then remembered his devil, and rushed home. When he reached his street, he smelled something burning, and saw smoke coming from his house. He stormed into his kitchen, where he found the devil sitting on the wooden floor. He had made an open fire and was roasting the neighbor's dog on a spit.

Of course, devils aren't really for sale, as we know. This story is just a dramatic way of teaching us something we ought to know about evil. We know all too well that we get into more trouble when we have nothing to do. It seems the dark side of us is always waiting for its opportunity to show itself, and that opportunity so often comes when our hands are idle and we have nothing constructive to do. This is when we are tempted to pick a fight, to destroy something that someone else has made, or to simply be mischievous.

That phrase from the Lord's Prayer—"and lead us not into temptation"—is one we repeat so often that we never give it a second thought. Perhaps we should make this request more consciously. And might we not also ask God to keep us busy all day doing what is positive and constructive? If we are busy for the Lord and his good, then we will in truth be delivered from all evil.

Note: A good story does not need to be explained. Since this is a good story, I hesitate to add any kind of explanation. But because of the stark images, I would target this sermon for older children/youth and include a warning that it is about the dark side of each of us.

A Prince in Disguise*

Text: Matthew 25:31-46 (44-45)
Appropriate Day: All Saints' Day, any Sunday
Summary: Treat everyone as if he were Jesus.

Preparation: Spend a few minutes discussing what a disguise is, and then read or summarize the Bible passage. The story will then have a context, and you won't need to interrupt it to offer explanation.

Today I want you to listen very carefully to a story. This story will not take the place of the usual children's sermon; it *is* the children's sermon because it has a double meaning. After I've finished it you'll have to think about it and perhaps ask your parents about its meaning. It's called "A Prince in Disguise."

Once, long ago (but not too long ago) in a faraway place (but not too far away), there lived a very special king. He was, by any standard, very kind, very just, and very wise. Even though his kingdom had no boundaries, for it was large beyond imagination, everyone in it knew the king was a loving father. Once a week he would step into his royal carriage, and his royal coachman and royal horses would carry him through the streets. And of course all the young men would bow and all the young ladies would curtsy as the king passed by.

Although this king was very, very rich, there was one thing he did not have, and because he did not have it, he wanted it

*Or princess, if you prefer.

115

more than anything else in the world. Can you guess what it was? That's right—he wanted a son. The king prayed every morning and every evening that a son would be born to him and his wife, the queen, for what good would his kingdom be if he did not have an heir who would become the next king? Oh, how he prayed and wished for a son.

And one day it happened: the queen gave birth to a child, and it was a boy! The good news spread quickly throughout the kingdom, and the people were happy and thankful; now there would be a prince who would someday be the next king.

The years passed, and the little baby boy grew to be a little prince. And once a week the prince and his father the king would step into the royal carriage, and the royal coachman and the royal horses would carry them through the streets.

Because the king had only one son and because he loved him with all his heart, he was especially careful to make sure that no harm would befall his son. In fact, he built a very tall stone wall around the castle so that the prince would see nothing of the ugly, evil things that happened in the world beyond it. But the prince was curious, just like boys and girls about your age, and one day he decided that he wanted to see what the world was like beyond the stone wall. After carefully disguising himself, he slipped away from the castle. He walked down dusty roads and through village streets. He saw the clear blue skies, enjoyed the beautiful flowers, and felt the gentle rain just as he did behind the stone wall; but he also saw people stealing and cheating one another, and mothers too poor to feed their babies.

Of course, the king was frantic when he discovered that his dearly beloved son was lost in the great world beyond the castle walls. So the king gathered together all his messengers and told them to go to every street corner and alleyway and read to the people this solemn declaration: My son, the prince, is lost somewhere among you. Will you help me find him?

Young and old, male and female, the people looked high and low to find the prince, because they knew the king would be forever grateful if they found his son. But no one could find the prince, because he had disguised himself to look just like everyone else. And because the prince could be anyone, the people decided it was best to treat everyone as if he were the prince.

Even to this very day the prince still walks the streets, and you may by chance meet him someday.

Note: I prefer to leave the story open-ended for the reasons discussed in "The Story as Proclamation" in Part I. The success of this story doesn't depend on its analogy to the story of Jesus in Matthew 25. It can stand by itself in the minds of younger children as a story of a prince who learns the truth about this world and of a father's love for his son. Older children and those adults who "happen" to be listening in will catch the analogy. True, our primary responsibility is to target children's sermons for children, but we should never forget the powerful dynamics that develop when others listen in. This is one very good reason why the Sunday Scripture lesson(s) should serve as the basis for both children and adult sermons.

Baa-Baa

Text: Luke 15:1-7 (". . . until he finds it")
Season: Any
Summary: God is like a good shepherd who searches until she finds the one who is lost.*
Props: A shepherd's crook; a flannel board and figures: a shepherd (male or female figure), a lamb and a flock of sheep, a sun, and a black piece of felt (or similar material) to represent the darkness.

If you have ever seen a real lamb, which is soft and cuddly, you can't help but want to give it a big hug. Have you ever thought what it would be like to be a little lamb? If you were a lamb, you would need someone to watch over you, someone to keep you from getting lost—a shepherd. And a shepherd might carry a crook like this one, which a friend (supply the name) lent me. The crook is used by shepherds both to ward off any would-be attackers, like a wolf, and to pull back a lamb if it begins to wander away. (Illustrate its use.) Like most children I know, lambs have a way of wandering off and becoming lost. If the shepherd sees this happening, she will use her crook and gently pull or nudge the lamb back toward the flock.

My story this morning is about a lamb named Baa-Baa who gets lost, and about a good shepherd. (Arrange the figures on the flannel board.) I'm telling this story because Jesus told a

---

*I have made the shepherd in this story a female because I believe that the feminine side of God is usually overshadowed by male images. I would also note that in the following parable, that of the lost coin, it is the woman who seeks diligently "until she finds it."

118

similar story when he wanted to explain what God is like. He said that God is like a shepherd who searches until she finds the one who is lost.

Our story begins on a day in spring. The sun was brightly shining, the clouds were puffy and white, and Baa-Baa was as happy as she could be. It was a beautiful day, and the grass was green and especially sweet. She never imagined that something could go wrong.

Baa-Baa thought to herself how nice it was to have a good shepherd to watch over the flock. Today she was leading them to a new field. Baa-Baa had never been here before, but then she had never been much of any place before. She noticed that the sun was not as high in the sky as it had been, which meant that it would soon be getting dark, but it didn't seem to matter. Baa-Baa just kept on munching the sweet grass, not even noticing that she was moving farther and farther away from the rest of the flock. And in no time at all Baa-Baa was eating grass all by herself.

It was quite a long time before Baa-Baa realized what had happened. The flock had gone off without her, or she had gone off without the flock. Whatever had happened, it was time to start looking for the other sheep. She tried very hard to find them, because she didn't want to be scolded for getting lost, but the harder she tried the more lost she became. Now it was getting dark, and Baa-Baa began thinking about all the terrible things that could happen to her. What if night came, and she was still lost? She might fall and break a leg, she would have nothing to drink, she would get cold, and the wolves—she didn't want to think about the wolves. It no longer mattered if the shepherd would scold her for getting lost; Baa-Baa just wanted to be found.

Then she thought, I wonder if the good shepherd is looking for me? Would she try to find me in the night? Would she leave the other sheep and come after me? Would she do that to find just one lamb?

Suddenly, darkness came in all its blackness (illustrate), and Baa-Baa couldn't see anything. There was nothing she could do but wait, wait and find out if the good shepherd cared enough to come looking for just one forgetful lamb that had gotten lost.

Baa-Baa had no idea what time it was when she heard a noise. Her first thought was that the wolves had found her. But then she heard someone calling her name: "Baa-Baa. Baa-Baa." She started running, trying to find the voice that called to her. Before she could see the shepherd, she heard footsteps —fast footsteps. And when at last the figure in the dark became clear, the shepherd was not only calling her name, but was running toward her. When she reached Baa-Baa she lifted her onto her shoulders.

They were on their way home now—Baa-Baa was sure of that. She also knew how good it felt to be safe again in the arms of one who loved her very much. Then Baa-Baa noticed that the good shepherd was carrying her crook. But this time she didn't need her crook; she had come herself to find one lost and lonely lamb.

And that is the end of the story, although it isn't really *my* story. It is Jesus' story, the one he told when he wanted to explain to others what God is like. God is like the good shepherd who will not rest until she finds you.

Note: I didn't try to build into this story an analogy between being lost and being "lost" in sin. Certainly this is part of the biblical account, but the sermon is focused on the single experience of knowing a God who cares enough to leave the ninety-nine in order to find the one that is lost.

THE PROPHETS

These sermons are intended to exemplify the meaning of the term "prophetic" in both biblical and contemporary settings.

A SPECIAL NOTE

Children's ideas about prophets are hazy at best. Most children think of them as men in long gowns who spoke the word of God. Though they may be able to name a prophet or two, they will not be able to distinguish Isaiah from Jeremiah. And though they may have a faint idea about why the prophets were important, they will probably not know what it means to be a prophetic church today.

Prophets were primarily those who took faith out of the temple and into the marketplace of human affairs. Needless to say, prophets, both male and female, did more *forth*-telling than *fore*-telling, and children ought to know that Martin Luther King, Jr., is part of the prophetic tradition in a way that Jeane Dixon is not.

Prophets also stood apart because of their double message of judgment *and* hope, so we should avoid depicting them in purely negative terms. When they spoke of God's pending judgment, they always balanced it with positive assurances: "God wants you to be his people: God believes you can be his light unto the nations. But if you persist in your ways . . ." (cf. Jer. 18:5ff.). The prophets also stressed the corporate —they were concerned about the redemption of the nation—so we must be careful not to individualize or trivialize their message.

I have included this special section on the prophets because I fear the Church is not raising up new prophets who know what it means to stand in the marketplace proclaiming God's message of liberation (judgment and hope). If we fail this generation, the next generation will pay the price.

122

How Will We Turn Out?

Text: Jeremiah 18:1-11*
Appropriate Day: Independence Day
Summary: God still has great hopes that America will be a shining example to other nations.
Props: Modeling clay and one piece of brittle clay

This morning I have brought with me a lump of modeling clay. If we had the time I would give each of you a lump of it to shape into a pot or a cup. I also wish I had a potter's wheel, because that would make it much easier to form this lump of clay into something useful. This is something most of you have probably seen—a potter shaping a pot as he sits at his turning wheel.

Before we go any further, let me read a passage from the book of Jeremiah that speaks about the art of pottery. (Read or summarize Jeremiah 18:1-11.)

When Jeremiah went down to the potter's house, he observed that when a pot made of soft clay turns out wrong, the potter simply throws it back on the wheel and starts again, shaping it until it is right. But if the clay has hardened and set, as this piece has, then the potter can do nothing with it. You see, it just crumbles in my hands. (Break brittle clay into pieces.) It is much easier to work with this lump of clay (knead fresh clay) because it is still moist and soft. (Continue working

*The first time I gave this sermon I interpreted the text in a personal manner: the clay was the lives of the children. But when I reread the text I knew I had done the prophet a great injustice, because one of the characteristics of a prophetic ministry is to interpret God's will in terms of nations and their leaders. My exegesis also made me see the thread of hope that runs through these chapters.

the clay into a pot. If this seems too difficult to do on the spot, get a good start on it beforehand. You can re-use this pot later in "Breaking Pots.")

These Bible verses suggest that we might think of America as a lump of soft, unshaped clay. God wants very much for America to be a beautifully shaped and useful pot, and he will help us become that, if we are willing. If we stop and think about it, we realize we can let God be the potter in many ways. We can treat all people equally, regardless of where they came from, how they look or speak, what color their skin is, or how much money they have. We can be generous when our land grows more food than we need. We can choose leaders who are good examples. And, finally, we can show courage enough to stand beside those nations that are struggling for their freedom and dignity.

You may be thinking that this is a lot to expect of America. And, of course, we have often fallen short of these high ideals. As boys and girls you know what it's like when you don't live up to your own expectations or the expectations of others. But we have to keep on trying. And we must also let God try and try again with us, because he has great expectations not only for each of us as individuals, but for *all* of us who live in America.

Since this is the Sunday before the Fourth of July, which is Independence Day, I've been thinking about the birth of our nation. And I've realized that ever since we won our freedom from England, the eyes of the world have been upon us. This is still very true today: the world watches every move we make to see if we mean what we say, and to see what kind of nation we are. You might say that the world is watching to see how we'll turn out. It's like the time that the prophet Jeremiah went down to the potter's house. This great nation of ours could turn out to be very beautiful, or it could become stubborn and brittle and be cast aside as useless.

Breaking Pots

Text: Jeremiah 19:1-11
Appropriate Day: Independence Day, any Sunday
Summary: A prophet is a person who is not afraid to tell the nation when it has stopped trusting in God.
Props: The clay pot previously made in "How Will We Turn Out?"

This morning I have two things I would like you to look at. The first one is a certain phrase that is inscribed on our coins. If anyone has a penny, a nickel, a dime, or a quarter, take it out and see if you can find the words "In God We Trust" on it. You'll have to look hard, because the print is small, but it's there.

Our nation, like the ancient nation of Israel, was formed at a time when its leaders and its people had put their trust in God. And the American people are like the Hebrew people in another important way. We both came into a promised land, a land flowing with milk and honey—in other words, a land that was good enough to give us enough food so that no one would need to go hungry. The pilgrims came across the ocean and the Hebrews crossed the Jordan River, and both nations began by believing that God could be trusted. And that is why you will find inscribed on our coins the phrase "In God We Trust."

The other thing I brought with me is this pot. Some of you may remember it as the pot I started to make as I was talking about the prophet Jeremiah. It's finished now, as you can see. (Show to children.) It has also become hard and brittle, which means that it will break easily. I hope you also remember that Jeremiah wanted the Hebrew nation of Judah to be like soft clay so that God could continue to shape her. But he was afraid that the people of Judah had become so hard and so brittle that they no longer trusted in God. They began to worship gods they made with their hands—called graven images—and they began to say to themselves "We will do whatever we want. We don't need God anymore. We don't need his commandments, and we don't need his forgiveness. If we want to depend upon our own strength to fight our enemies, we will do just that."

I would like you to think with me for a moment about this question: Does America still trust in God? Do our leaders, do the people of _____ (name your city), do you and I forget God? Do we say to ourselves in so many words, "We will do whatever *we* think is right. We don't need God anymore; we can get along very well without him. We're strong enough to defend ourselves." (Pause to give the children time to reflect on these questions).

Jeremiah believed he knew the answer to these questions for his country of Judah. You might say that he was more than unhappy with the people and their leaders—he was angry!

I want you to keep in mind that a prophet is someone who is not afraid to stand up and speak out when he knows a sacred agreement with God has been broken. This is what a prophet does, regardless of the time in which he lives. Jeremiah spoke and he preached, but no one would listen to his words. And so Jeremiah took a clay pot—a pot like this one that's hard and can no longer be reshaped—and he said to the people of Judah, "Since you will not hear my words, I give you this sign of warning. Either you trust in God or, like this pot, you will be broken into pieces and scattered across the land." (Break your pot. It might be best to use a hammer.)

(Now that you have everyone's attention, don't moralize.) Breaking an agreement with God is serious business. Have we broken our covenant with God?

Note: Be alert to the danger of identifying America with Israel. We are a nation of Christians but not necessarily heirs to the Covenant (the Church is, perhaps, but not the United

States). Prophets must speak to the nation as well as to the Church, but not always from the same assumption or claims. Being a nation in which Christians are a majority does not make us a Christian nation. Thus in many cases the prophet will speak the same imperative to nation and Church but not always from the same indicative.

Jim, the Promise-Mender

Text: Hosea 1:2; 2:19-23
Appropriate Day: Any Sunday
Summary: A prophet is someone who makes us remember a promise we made with God.
Props: Handwritten signs bearing the messages mentioned below (post them as you are telling the story)

We have all had the experience of making a promise with someone. If it was a very, very important promise, we may remember how it turned out—was the promise remembered and kept, or forgotten and never kept?

Promises we know about; prophets we aren't so sure about. The story I tell you now is of a boy and a promise and how he became a prophet.

Jim was looking forward to the special fishing trip he and his father had talked about several weeks ago. His father had promised they could go on Saturday. Today was only Monday, but Jim was making sure his fishing pole was ready to go—even though his father hadn't said anything more about the trip. When Saturday morning came, Jim got up early and went into his father's bedroom to wake him up. "Dad, it's time to get up," Jim whispered in his ear. "We're going fishing, remember?"

"Fishing trip?" his dad questioned by the tone of his voice. "What fishing trip?"

"The one you promised," answered Jim.

"I don't remember making any promise," his father said.

Jim's heart sank. He went back to his room, and as he sat on the edge of his bed, he could feel his disappointment turning to anger. "How could my father forget?" he wondered. If only he could get his father to remember his promise. Then Jim had an idea. He would tape various signs where his father would be sure to see them.

Half an hour later, Jim had posted his signs. On the car the sign read "Going Fishing"; on the refrigerator door, "Monday, April 21" (that was the day his father had made the promse). The sign on his father's desk said "Bowe Lake." But the biggest sign of all he taped to his father's bedroom door. It read "Promise-Breaker." But there was no change. The signs came down and his father said nothing.

That night Jim prayed to God. Perhaps that is why the next morning he made a new sign—a sign that covered his father's bedroom door. It read "I Love You!"

When his father sat down for Sunday breakfast, he called Jim to join him. "Jim," he said with a twinkle in his eyes, "I couldn't help noticing the new sign on my door that says, 'I love you.' I guess it means you aren't angry with me anymore. And I have a confession to make. The fishing trip we missed—I do remember the promise. I had forgotten about it, and then I wasn't Christian enough to admit I had forgotten it. I was a promise-breaker. But you and your sign made me want very much to remember. Can we start again and make a new promise agreement—one that I will be sure to remember?"

My story of Jim the promise-mender is also a story of Jim the prophet, because prophets are like Jim. They get angry when we break the promises we've made with God. Prophets long ago got angry when Israel forgot, or simply didn't care, about the promises she had made with God. But they also told the people of Israel that God still loved them. Prophets today are also like Jim when they remind us about the promises we have made to help the poor and make the world a safe place to live.

And, just like Jim, you can be a prophet in your own way. I know you will speak up when someone you love breaks their promise to you. And please speak up, too, when you believe any of us who are Christians are not keeping our promises to God.

Note: We usually compare contemporary role models with biblical models (". . . because Jim is like an Old Testament prophet"), but in this story I reversed the comparison (". . . because Old Testament prophets are like Jim"). Because this story is targeted for younger children, I began it with a contemporary example, which they can understand without a historical framework. I also made a conscious effort, particularly because of the target age, to avoid the sticky business of making prophets the conscience of the nation. (See the Note in "Breaking Pots": America as a nation has not necessarily entered into a covenantal promise with God—at least not by popular vote.)

POSTSCRIPT

Since this book is about creativity as much as it is about theology, I would appreciate hearing from you. We share creativity not so much to copy or reproduce it but to spark the creative spirit within all of us. God's grace and love have touched your life in a different way than they have touched mine. In discussing lifestyles, Henry Thoreau stated it this way:

> I would not have anyone adopt *my* mode of living on any account; for, beside that before he has fairly learned it I may have found out another for myself, I desire that there may be as many different persons in the world as possible; but I would have each one be very careful to find out and pursue *his own* way. . . .

Correspondence—ideas about experiments, successes and failures, sermons, stories, Gospel participations, and so forth —may be mailed to this address:

Community Church of Durham
   Box U
      Durham, New Hampshire 03824

BIBLIOGRAPHY
and Other Related Readings

Preaching, Storytelling, and Parables

Buechner, Frederick. *Telling the Truth: The Gospel as Tragedy, Comedy & Fairy Tale*. New York: Harper & Row, 1977.

Buechner, Frederick. "The Two Stories," a commencement address. Published in Bangor Theological Seminary's *Open Door*, Summer 1980.

Coleman, Richard J. "What Aggravates Me About the Preaching I Hear," *The Pulpit*, December 1968.

Craddock, Fred B. *Overhearing the Gospel*. Nashville: Abingdon, 1978.

Crossan, John Dominic. *In Parables*. New York: Harper & Row, 1973.

Jensen, Richard A. *Telling the Story*. Minneapolis: Augsburg, 1980.

Jeremias, Joachim. *The Parables of Jesus*. New York: Charles Scribner's Sons, 1963; rev. ed. 1971.

Sanders, James A. *God Has a Story Too*. Philadelphia: Fortress Press, 1979.

Scherer, Paul. *The Word God Sent*. New York: Harper & Row, 1965.

Shea, John. *Stories of God: An Unauthorized Biography*. Chicago: Thomas More Press, 1978.

Wilder, Amos. *Early Christian Rhetoric: The Language of the Gospel*. Cambridge: Harvard University Press, 1971.

Faith and Moral Development; Education as Transformation

Bettelheim, Bruno. *The Uses of Enchantment*. New York: Alfred A. Knopf, 1976.

Cully, Iris V. *Christian Child Development*. San Francisco: Harper & Row, 1979. Cully includes theories of Erikson, Piaget, Bruner, and Goldman and their application to religious education.

Donaldson, Margaret. *Children's Minds*. New York: W. W. Norton & Company, 1978.

Duska, Ronald, and Mariellen Whelan. *Moral Development: A Guide to Piaget and Kohlberg*. New York: Paulist Press, 1975.

Fowler, James W. *Stages of Faith: The Psychology of Human Development and the Quest for Meaning*. San Francisco: Harper & Row, 1981. This book also includes a good discussion of the nature of faith.

Fowler, Jim, and Sam Keen. *Life Maps: Conversations on the Journey to Faith*. Waco, Texas: Word Books, 1978. This book includes Fowler's initial and abbreviated theory of faith development.

Groome, Thomas. *Christian Religious Education: Sharing Our Story and Vision.* San Francisco: Harper & Row, 1980.

Loder, James E. *The Transforming Moment: Understanding Convictional Experiences.* San Francisco: Harper & Row, 1981. Like Groome and Fowler, Loder develops a sophisticated theory concerning Christian transformation.

Westerhoff, John H. *Bringing up Children in the Christian Faith.* Minneapolis: Winston Press, 1980.

Wink, Walter. *Transforming Bible Study.* Nashville: Abingdon, 1980. The author's methodology for teaching the Bible has implications for teaching and transforming in general.

Worship

Abernethy, William B. *A New Look for Sunday Morning.* Nashville: Abingdon, 1975. This is the story of a church's attempt to interweave worship, religious education, and celebration.

Cully, Iris V. *Christian Worship and Church Education.* Philadelphia: Westminster Press, 1967. The educational task of the church is described within the priority of worship.

Emswiler, Thomas N., and Sharon N. Emswiler. *Wholeness in Worship.* San Francisco: Harper & Row, 1980. This book includes creative models for Sunday, family, and special services.

Ng, David, and Virginia Thomas. *Children in the Worshipping Community.* Atlanta: John Knox Press, 1981. The authors seek a balance between theological integrity and relevance for children.

Westerhoff, John H. *Will Our Children Have Faith?* New York: Seabury Press, 1976. The author wants to replace the "schooling-instructional" method with a "community-of-faith" enculturation.

White, James F. *Introduction to Christian Worship.* Nashville: Abingdon, 1980.

Miscellaneous

Bonhoeffer, Dietrich. *Letter and Papers from Prison.* Ed. Eberhard Bethge. New York: Macmillan, 1953.

Levinson, Daniel J. *The Seasons of a Man's Life.* New York: Alfred A. Knopf, 1978.

Lynn, Robert W., and Elliott Wright. *The Big Little School: Two Hundred Years of the Sunday School.* Nashville: Abingdon, 1971.

McGinnis, Kathleen, and James McGinnis. *Parenting for Peace and Justice.* Maryknoll, N.Y.: Orbis Books, 1981. The authors explore teaching within a family context. A workbook, a filmstrip, and tapes are available for a church-wide program. This book provides an excellent integration of social action, education, and the intergenerational approach to the exploration of faith.

BIBLIOGRAPHY AND OTHER RELATED READINGS

Quoist, Michael. *Prayers*. New York: Sheed & Ward, 1963.

Sanders, James A. *Torah and Canon*. Philadelphia: Fortress Press, 1972.

Sheehy, Gail. *Passages*. New York: E. P. Dutton & Co., 1974.

Von Rad, Gerhard. *Old Testament Theology*. 2 vols. New York: Harper & Row, 1962.